Giulia Castelli Gattinara

111 Places in Milan That You Must Not Miss

Photographs by Mario Verin

emons:

© Emons Verlag GmbH
All rights reserved
© Photographs: Mario Verin
cover icon: fotolia.com © Wolfgang Jargstorff
Design: Eva Kraskes, based on a design
by Lübbeke | Naumann | Thoben
Maps: altancicek.design, www.altancicek.de
English translation: Thomas Fazi
Edited by Katrina Fried
Printing and binding: Grafisches Centrum Cuno, Calbe
Printed in Germany 2015
ISBN 978-3-95451-331-4
First edition

Did you enjoy it? Do you want more?
Join us in uncovering new places around the world on:
www.111places.com

Foreword

Ambitious, trendy, and creative on all fronts: we are speaking of the *Milano da bere* ("Drinkin' Milan"), as the city's yuppie nightlife was known in the eighties. Milan is a city that works hard by day and parties even harder by night. Start with an aperitif in Brera, the artists' district, and then move on to the Navigli – the system of canals designed in part by Leonardo da Vinci – for a "chic 'n quick" meal. Milan is at once traditional and bold – a city that dons its finest evening dress for the opening night of La Scala, but has the audacity to install a 36-foot-high sculpture of a middle finger pointing straight at the city's stock market.

Well-cultured, elegant, exclusive – just as one would expect the country's financial capital to be – Milan is at its best when it turns into a top-class international fashion and design showcase. With its ambitious 26-story "vertical forest" now completed, the city has radically altered its skyline in just a few years – even going so far as to place a replica of the *Madonnina* (Little Madonna – the statue of the Virgin Mary that towers over the Duomo) – on top of the Pirelli Tower, its highest skyscraper. From flamingo-filled courtyards to old warehouses turned contemporary art workshops, the city can be as surprising and bizarre as the Art Nouveau-style façades of its buildings.

Milan is a metropolis that doesn't show off – you have to go looking for it, landmark by landmark. Whether you search for its essence in the backstage of a theater or the vault of a bank, you will not be disappointed.

111 Places

1__770

The rabbi's house

It's not a number from the Jewish Kabbalah, although it evokes that kind of atmosphere. The curious story of "House 770" begins in New York City, in a Flemish-style house located at 770 Eastern Parkway in the Crown Heights neighborhood of Brooklyn, to be precise. It's not the kind of place where you would expect to find a typical Dutch house. But Americans are an eclectic and relatively young people – which is why they like to "pick and mix" from Europe's rich architectural history. They are also an immigrant nation, which explains why the Lubavitchers, a group of Orthodox Jews originally from Belarus, chose the typical European-looking house, originally used as a medical center, for Rabbi Joseph Isaac Schneersohn (1880–1950), who was forced to cross the Atlantic to flee Nazi persecution in 1940. They wanted him to feel more at home.

Over time, the rabbi's synagogue, office, and residence became a focal point for the local Hasidic community. So much so that at some point the wealthy Lubavitchers set out to build 770 replicas of the Gothic-style Brooklyn dwelling in different locations around the world. The defining architectural details of these near duplicates are the redbrick façade, the three roof gables, the baldachin that overlooks the front door, and the marble decorations beneath the ground-floor windows.

Ultimately, however, there were only 12 replicas built (one of which is in Jerusalem): some are surrounded by ample gardens, such as those in Montreal, Canada, and Melbourne, Australia; others are squeezed between high-rises, like the one in São Paulo, Brazil. There are also a few elsewhere in the United States, including New Jersey and California. Though there are some small differences between the various buildings, from afar they appear practically identical.

In Italy there is only one example of House 770, and it is in Milan. It also serves as a synagogue.

Address Via Carlo Poerio 35, 20129 Milan | Getting there Porta Venezia (M2 red line); Bixio (tram 23) | Tip Next to House 770, a plaque pays homage to the house of Mario Rollier and his wife (a Waldensian couple), where on August 27th, 1943, the founding congress of the European Federalist movement was held. A number of notable anti-fascists of the time were present, including Franco Venturi, Altiero Spinelli, Ernesto Rossi, Leone Ginzburg, and Willy Jervis.

2　Aldo Coppola
A haircut in the clouds

A magnificent view is not normally what you think about when choosing a hair salon. But at Aldo Coppola that's exactly what you'll get. Located on the eighth floor of the Rinascente building, at the height of the Duomo's steeples, Aldo Coppola's beauty salon – the number one of its kind in Milan and a favorite among celebrities and the fashion set – looks straight out upon the enormous cathedral's stunning array of pinnacles, buttresses, gargoyles, and statuettes. Make yourself comfortable, and let Milan's most exclusive hair stylists – known for creating geometric hair designs no less daring than the Duomo's own Gothic sculptures – work their magic.

You can choose to gaze into the mirror and follow the artist's work step by step – as he or she masterfully cuts, dyes, perms, or highlights your hair – or you can turn your head and admire the squeaky-clean marble that adorns the ornate cathedral beyond the large glass window panes.

In wintertime, immerse yourself in the protective warmth of the room's mirrors, steel, and designer armchairs, safe in the knowledge that you will walk out the door more beautiful and chic than ever. In spring and summer, experience a haircut on the salon's lovely sun-drenched terrace, and enjoy a cup of tea or frothy latté and a friendly chat amid the clouds. *Voilà*: what is usually an exercise in female patience – waiting for your highlighting process to be over or for your hair dye to sink in – has turned into an experience that you wish would never end.

A place for all women this is not: you need to be daring, bold, and fairly well-heeled – but offer your head as a canvas to Stefano Lorenzi and Adalberto Vanoni, the atelier's two creative directors, and you will emerge transformed and renewed. If you don't feel quite ready to commit yourself, you can always simply drop by for a peek, or to browse the salon's line of hair care products.

Address Piazza Duomo (left side), Rinascente building (8th floor), 20121 Milan,
Tel +39 0289059712, www.aldocoppola.it | Getting there Duomo (M1 red line,
M1 green line) | Hours Mon–Sun 10am–9pm | Tip On the 7th floor is the Rinascente's
terrace bar. It gets very noisy on Tuesdays and Thursdays, when live music is played at an
ear-splitting volume (Mon–Sun 9am–10pm, 9am–midnight in the summer).

3 ___ The Ambrosiana

The "democratic" library of Cardinal Borromeo

From Umberto Eco's *The Name of the Rose* to Dan Brown's *The Da Vinci Code*, in our collective imagination a library like the Ambrosiana is bound to be a place of mystery and intrigue. Yet this place's history is rather different. This is where Cardinal Federico Borromeo first revealed to the public the Church's secular knowledge. He sent twelve apostles across Europe, Greece, and Flanders in search of the rarest and most precious books of the time, most of which we can still admire today in all their ancient leather-bound and gold-stamped beauty.

To reach the Sala Federiciana, the ancient reading room of the library, you have to pass through the Pinacoteca (the art gallery), and it's well worth the walk – Raffaello, Caravaggio, Tiziano, Leonardo, and Brueghel are just some of the illustrious artists whose paintings adorn its walls. The library was inaugurated in 1609 as a place of culture open to everyone. Here the progressive cardinal, quoted even by Manzoni, would receive and converse with the most eminent scholars of his age. It's easy to imagine the scholars' stupor at the sight of thousands of immensely rare volumes – delivered here by way of long and perilous journeys – such as Plauto's verses (2nd century BC) transcribed in fragments dating back to the 5th century; or the Gospel of the Arian bishop Ulfilas, written in Gothic (4th century AD); and even a priceless copy of Aristotle's *Nicomachean Ethics*, with marginalia by Boccaccio and Virgil, miniature paintings by Simone Martini, and annotations by Petrarca.

In 1943, the Sala Federiciana was engulfed by a fire, much like the Library of Alexandria centuries earlier, and many of the cinquecentine (books printed in the 16th century) were lost. Most of them survived, though, and can today be accessed in digital form. Leonardo da Vinci's *Atlantic Codex*, for example, is viewable on a touch screen.

Address Piazza Pio XI 2, 20123 Milan, Tel +39 02806921, www.ambrosiana.eu |
Getting there Cordusio (M 1 red line; tram 2, 12, 14, 16, 27); Duomo (M 3 yellow
line) | Hours Tue – Sun 10am – 6pm | Tip The church of San Sepolcro (19th century),
in the square behind the library, was rebuilt after the First Crusade (at the end of
1000 ad) in the same shape as its namesake in Jerusalem. It also appears in some
sketches by Leonardo da Vinci.

4_ Baladin

"Open source" beer

Teo Musso is originally from the Piedmont region, a land known for its wine but rather lacking when it comes to beer. So one day Musso and his partner decided to open a small tavern to sell their brand of home-brewed beer, the Baladin – a brew as cheerful as its creator. At first it wasn't that great, Musso admits. But over time, through sheer perseverance, he became a true *biermeister*. His philosophy – *baladin* means "acrobat" in French – is inspired by street theater, such as that of his friends' company, Cirque Bidon.

Musso is a globetrotter, himself, and from his first tavern-tent in Piozzo, in the province of Cuneo – where it all began in 1996 – he went on to open a string of breweries in Italy, Morocco, and New York. In each place he experimented with new techniques, juggled new ideas and regenerated his spirit. And so, over the years, Baladin has become a very successful brand based on an important ground rule: first and foremost, maintaining a healthy relationship with Mother Earth, because that is the essence of any good beer. Without compromising quality, Baladin has established itself as a household name on the Italian foodie scene, and in 2014 was awarded the title of best Italian home-brewed beer.

Currently, Baladin comes in 30 different varieties: ales, lagers, stouts, and malts, as well as coffee- and chocolate-scented beers – Musso's imagination knows no limits. There are also four "open source" beers – an homage to collective endeavors and the free movement of ideas. Anyone interested may consult the recipes on the company's website.

So head down to Via Solferino, to one of the latest Baladins to open in town, and indulge your thirst. Beneath the red brick arch, a 1950s-style girl drawn on the wall screams: "We just want beer!" This is the new 21st-century "Drinkin' Milan": less unscrupulous and more eco-friendly. Which is why we love it so much.

Address Via Solferino 56, 20121 Milan, Tel +39 026597758, www.baladin.it | **Getting there** Repubblica (M1 red line); Moscova (M2 green line); Monte Grappa / Gioia (tram 33) | **Tip** At Via Adelaide Ristori 2 there is another Baladin, called Bidenbum, which offers top-notch wines in addition to the usual selection of home-brewed beers.

5__ Bar Martini

Dolce & Gabbana's haute couture aperitif

You too can experience the glamour of Milan's famous high-fashion district at the Bar Martini, owned by Dolce & Gabbana. Opened in 2003, it is the result of a "merger" between two of Milan's most renowned brands.

The bar, just a stone's throw from San Babila, opens onto Corso Venezia through an arcade that leads to a historic 18th-century palazzo. You can also access it directly from the D&G men's store – just pass the shelves of polished black shoes, bags, and ties, until you reach the cafe tables in the winter garden, enclosed by glass and plants. The design is refined and deliberately minimalist, perfect for a quick break, a cup of coffee, or a snack with colleagues.

There is a certain pleasure that comes from ordering a hamburger – ironically called the "Big Martini," a reference to the famous McDonald's burger, though made with "quality beef," as the waiter points out – in such a lush setting. The Milanese are always in a hurry at lunchtime, but they still like to be served in style – and that is what the young, all-male staff at Bar Martini strives to offer. Here appearances really do count, and how could it be otherwise?

The atmosphere in the bar is classic D&G, dominated by the color black. The haute couture aperitif, the Dolce & Gabbana Martini cocktail, was created specifically to blend in with the leather sofas and dim-lit ambience created by the designer Ferruccio Laviani. A red dragon dominates the mosaic floor, while a red lampshade, made from Murano glass, descends from the ceiling like a flaming sun.

Even swankier – and pricier – is the Martini Bistrot. The restaurant is a flamboyant tribute to the sumptuous Milanese bars of the 1950s, complete with red velvet chairs, damasked panels, and gold-framed mirrors designed by Gio Ponti – all for the sole purpose of astonishing the eye and seducing the palate with a combination of Mediterranean tastes and international creativity.

Address Corso Venezia 15, 20122 Milan, Tel +39 0276011154 | Getting there San Babila or Palestro (M1 red line | Hours Mon–Sat 7:30–1am, Sun 9–midnight | Tip The Casa Fontana-Silvestri, at Corso Venezia 10, is one of the best preserved palaces of the Renaissance, to which the terra-cotta decorations of the façade are testament. You can't go in, but through the gate you can just about make out the *loggia*.

6__ The Barchett

The Naviglio as it would have been a century ago

The Darsena, the city's commercial port up until 1913, is today the heart of Milan's nightlife: it is here, in the many bars along the Naviglio Pavese and the Naviglio Ticinese, that the Milanese meet up after sunset. The atmosphere hasn't actually changed that much over time. The shouts of the porters loading and unloading cargo, the passengers disembarking from Abbiategrasso or Boffalora, the inquisitive glances of the customers – all this has simply made way for a new melting pot of faces and voices.

What's missing is the announcement of the departure of the *barchett*, the ferryboat that floated toward Milan by using the current, but had to be towed by a horse in the opposite direction. A century later the association Navigli Lombardi decided to put it back into action. The 5 to 8 hours of navigation have been reduced to 90 minutes, but this is more than enough time to view the urban landscape from a wholly different perspective: the city as seen from the river. There are many signs that remind one of the ferry's journey: the stone walls worn down by the chafing of the horses' ropes, the locks that regulated the different levels of water, the church of St. Christopher with its jetty for the passengers heading toward the city. Not to mention the passageway under the Scodellino Bridge that leads to the Darsena, the real heart of the Navigli system, linking it to the internal circuit.

The ring road connecting Via Fatebenefratelli, Via Senato, Via Santa Sofia, and Via Carducci (we are right in the city's center, after all, in the "limited traffic zone") is none other than the old waterway dating back to the 12th century, which was used in the 15th century by the engineers of the Fabbrica del Duomo to transport marble from Lago Maggiore to the building site of the new cathedral, via the Naviglio Grande. A fact that makes a ride on the *barchett* all the more exciting.

Address Alzaia Naviglio Grande 4, 20144 Milan, Tel +39 0292273118, www.navigareinlombardia.it | **Getting there** Porta Genova (M2 green line); Cantore (tram 19, 14; bus 47, 74) | **Hours** Open Apr–Sep and Christmas Day, consult the website for times | **Tip** In the gardens of Via Conca del Naviglio, you can see the Conca di Viarenna, built in the 15th century to link the Naviglio Grande to the internal circuit, later replaced by the present Darsena.

7__ The Boxer's Spire

Strange encounters on the roof of the Duomo

You would probably never have guessed that there's a boxing match represented on one of the spires of the cathedral. It is not an allegory, but the celebration of the real-life boxer, Primo Carnera, who on June 26, 1933, became the first Italian to win the world heavyweight championship.

So it was that the anonymous sculptor of the Veneranda Fabbrica del Duomo, while restoring one of the spires, got the order to dedicate his work to the champion, engraving the event in the exquisite marble from Candoglia. Perhaps it was Mussolini himself who suggested it, seeing as Il Duce amply exploited the performances of the athlete nicknamed "the good giant" (Carnera was over 6.5 feet in height and weighed 265 pounds), transforming him into a poster boy for Fascist propaganda. Keeping the marble Carnera company is another famous boxer, Erminio Spalla.

Today, when you look up from the piazza towards the terraces to admire the spires that stand out against the sky, chiseled and adorned with statues and decorations, you would think that you are looking solely at biblical figures. Strange to think that in the midst of all those heavenly inlays and marble figures there is such an earthly, carnal scene as a fight between two boxers (complete with gloves).

And that is not the only surprise awaiting the trained eye: the spires are particularly susceptible to erosion by the elements and require constant maintenance, which often modifies the original iconography. If you climb up to the cathedral's roof, you can see this clearly. Think of it as a treasure hunt: among the figures of saints, demons, and garlands you can find a tennis racket and ball, or the semi-nude figure of a girl about to step down from her marble pedestal to join her lover, who is about to undertake the same stunt from the opposite side. Anything can happen under the watchful eye of the Madonnina.

Address Entrance to the Terrazze del Duomo, Piazza Duomo (on the left side),
20122 Milan, www.duomomilano.it | Getting there Duomo (M 1 red line; M 3 yellow
line); Torino (tram 2, 14); Duomo (tram 16, 12, 27) | Hours Mon – Sun 9am – 6:30pm,
May – Sep, Fri – Sat until 10pm | Tip With a donation you can "adopt" a spire and have
your name engraved on the cathedral (adottaunaguglia.duomomilano.it).

8_ Ca' de Ciapp

The scantily clad ladies of the Columbus Clinic

What are the statues of two half-naked women in unmistakably provocative poses doing on the façade – although thankfully not the front one – of the pious Columbus Clinic, which has its own chapel, a crucifix in every room, and is inspired by the principles of none other than the Missionaries of the Sacred Heart? Well, it's a funny story.

It all began at the dawn of the last century, when a wealthy entrepreneur, Ermenegildo Castiglioni, hired one of the most fashionable architects of the time, Giuseppe Sommaruga, to design his house in the center of Milan. Castiglioni wanted a residence that would be like no other, and sure enough, once it was completed in 1903 it became the "manifesto" of the Milanese Art Nouveau scene.

Built in raw ashlar masonry, in line with the new style's preference for naturalistic-looking elements, and overflowing with decorative stucco work, it also sported the statues of two scantily clad women, created by sculptor Ernesto Bazzaro, right above the main entrance. Predictably, the idea of these ladies showing off their backsides on one of the city's most aristocratic streets caused quite an uproar. Among the local folk, the stately building instantly came to be known as *Ca' de Ciapp* ("Buttocks House"). In 1914, the curvaceous statues were finally removed and relocated to another building also designed by Sommaruga, Villa Romeo Faccanoni in the Fiera district – which, ironically, became a Sacred Heart clinic in the 1940s.

Today the statues can be seen on the façade facing the garden. The pair of ladies are supposed to symbolize Peace and Industry, but their salaciousness is hard to deny – they *do* reveal their breasts and derrieres to the passersby after all. In any case, the surrounding garden offers many more innocent sights as well: butterflies, bees, and the many friezes adorning the lamps and handrails.

Address Via Michelangelo Buonarroti 48, 20145 Milan | **Getting there** Buonarroti (M 1 line); Giulio Cesare (bus 68) | **Tip** Palazzo Castiglioni, where the statues originally used to be, is at Corso Venezia 47. Today it houses the offices of the Italian General Confederation of Enterprises (*Confcommercio*). Take a stroll inside to see the monumental staircase and the sumptuous "peacock room," with its many friezes and polychrome decorations.

9__ Ca' dell'Oreggia

The ear-shaped intercom

Locals affectionately call it *Ca' dell'Oreggia* ("Ear House" in Milanese dialect) – a reference to the bronze ear-shaped intercom placed next to the front door. It was created by Adolf Wildt (1868–1931), a sculptor who specialized in auricles, but it is unknown where the Sola-Busca house's designer, Aldo Andreani (1887–1971), got the unusual idea.

Predictably, the object became the focus of countless urban legends. According to one of the most popular, ever since the *oreggia* ("ear") that functioned as the doorbell-intercom (one of the first in the city) stopped working, it acquired the magical power to make wishes come true, as long as you whisper into the patinaed earhole without being noticed by anyone.

Being an architect in Milan during the interwar years must have been a lot of fun. This period's style is known as "eclectic" – an attempt to classify an architectural aesthetic that defies categorization. It was a time in which strange figures started appearing on the city's façades, and architects felt at ease to move freely among all sorts of different designs and styles – medieval, classical, Art Nouveau, you name it – creating a melting pot of different cultures and epochs, as also testified to by a number of other buildings in the neighborhood (known as the Zone of Silence) including the Palazzo Castiglioni, at Corso Venezia 47, and Casa Berri-Meregalli, on Via Cappuccini.

Andreani had received a strictly classical education from the Polytechnic University of Milan and was second to none when it came to architectural history; he was a great connoisseur of the rationalist and avant-garde movements, and his models were Giulio Arata and Giuseppe Sommaruga. And yet, he had a poetic vision that drove him to indulge in daring experimentations – at least as far as his clients allowed him to, that is.

Address Via Gabrio Serbelloni 10, 20122 Milan | Getting there Palestro (M 1
red line); Monforte Donizetti (bus 54, 61) | Tip On Via Mozart at the corner of Luigi
Melegari is Palazzo Fidia, a structure so imaginative and ambitious that Andreani was
able to see only one of the four building designs that were part of his original concept
built; the remaining three were assigned to different architects, who reworked
Andreani's designs in a more sober fashion.

10___Ca' Granda

Learning in the University's courtyards

Ca' granda ("big house" in Milanese dialect) was once the nickname for the Ospedale Maggiore. The building, designed in the second half of the 15th century by Florentine architect Antonio Filarete, originally housed one of the first community hospitals. It was commissioned by the Duke of Milan, Francesco Sforza, and is among the first examples of Renaissance architecture in Northern Italy. Today it hosts the State University of Milan. The exterior, with an elegant sequence of arches and double lancet windows overlooking Via Festa del Perdono, has remained unchanged. The building's design splendidly combines the geometric rigor of Florentine Renaissance with the virtuosity of Gothic style. The latter is exemplified by the marble heads protruding above the arched windows, some of which are rather funny, such as one depicting a woman who appears to have received the fright of her life.

In his *Treatise on Architecture*, written between 1460 and 1464, Filarete offered a detailed outline of his project, inspired by the austere rationalism of Renaissance architecture. But he passed away before he completed the building. Those who took on the work added a touch of Gothic exuberance to the edifice. Students barely take notice nowadays, but the Richini courtyard, with its double arches, is truly monumental. Were it not for its geometric rigidity, the building could easily be mistaken for a royal palace.

So take a stroll through the four cloisters as you make your way toward the departments of history and philosophy. The first two, called *della Ghiacciaia* ("Icehouse cloister") and *della Legnaia* ("Woodhouse cloister") – a reference to the roman relics that were recovered here – were destroyed during World War II and had to be rebuilt; the other two, on the Western side, called *dei Bagni* ("Toilets cloister") and *della Farmacia* ("Pharmacy cloister"), are the original 15th-century structures.

Address Via Festa del Perdono 7, 20122 Milan | **Getting there** Cordusio (M 1 red line); Missori and Crocetta (M 3 yellow line); Romana / Santa Sofia (tram 16, 24), Vittorio (tram 12, 23, 27; bus 60, 73, 84) | **Tip** The crypt of the Church of Santa Maria Annunziata (accessible from the University's Richini courtyard) is where the bodies of the patriots who died during the Five Days of Milan revolt were originally buried, before being moved to the mausoleum in Piazza Cinque Giornate. The names of the victims are still inscribed on the wall.

11__The Cannocchiale
A view through the arches

The Milanese affectionately refer to it as the *Cannocchiale* ("telescope"): a view across Parco Sempione (Simplon Park) from the Arco della Pace (Arch of Peace) all the way to the Castello Sforzesco (Sforza Castle), which is striking from any vantage point. From the southern end, the view is framed by a succession of medieval portals. At the northern end, the neoclassical triumphal arch by Luigi Cagnola glistens in marble splendor. The arch's design was modeled after the Arco Septimius Severus in the Roman Furum. Given its central location, families from all over the city gather here on Sundays to stroll through the surrounding gardens.

It is a local Milanese tradition for fathers to sit under the arch and tell their children the complicated history of the Italian Risorgimento. Construction of the monument began in 1807 to celebrate Napoleon's victories, and was originally named the Arco delle Vittorie (Arch of Victory). History had other plans, though, and the triumphal arch ended up honoring the peace treaty between Italy and Austria after the Congress of Vienna in 1815. The significance of that event is symbolized by the magnificent bronze *sestiga* (a chariot drawn by six horses) on top of the monument, designed by Abbondio Sangiorgio. The six horses originally faced north, toward France, but, as events took a different turn, they were repositioned to face the opposite direction.

The *Cannocchiale* has a lot of stories to tell, but what children remember most is its curious perspective. And understandably so: the sight is a real eye-catcher, spanning both the city's monuments as well as its history, from the ancient Duchy of Savoy to the arch through which the French armies marched. What fun for them to imagine the medieval knights riding out from the Sforza Castle and trotting through the gardens with their colorful banners and heavy armor.

Address Largo Benedetto Cairoli (southern end), Piazza Sempione (northern end), 20154 Milan | **Getting there** Cairoli-Castello (M1 red line; tram 1); Arco della Pace (tram 1, 19) | **Hours** Tue and Thu 9:30am–2:30pm, Wed and Fri 2–7pm, Sat 10:30am–6:30pm | **Tip** In the center of the park (Via Cervantes), there is a 1950s pavilion, which houses a civic library. The decorations are by the artist Bruno Munari.

12 Casa Degli Omenoni

Where the owner was friends with Michelangelo

Six male figures decorate the facade of this 16th-century palazzo designed by Leone Leoni. The sculptor moved to Milan in 1542 in search of a house. He ended up having one built instead, and he asked Antonio Abbondio, a well-known Lombard artist, to design the six stone telamons that dominate the façade.

Locals began to refer to them as the *Omenomi* ("large men"), and as time went by, both the palazzo and the street came to be known by this name. Sad and pensive, with their curly beards and low-hanging heads, they represent the defeated barbarians. Telamons are decorative structural supports that originated in Magna Graecia, the coastal area of Southern Italy on the Tarentine Gulf that was once populated by Greek settlers. The colossi in the Temple of Zeus, in Agrigento, are one example. The passersby, however, most likely ignored this fact, as well as the reference to the myth of Atlas, the Titan who carried the world on his shoulders.

That said, it is likely that Leoni was more inspired by the dynamic male figures sculpted by his friend Michelangelo for the Roman tomb of Pope Julius II. Leoni, in fact, had in his studio the *Quadrone dei Giganti* by the Florentine artist. In his day, Leoni's home was a veritable museum, displaying various works of art by some of his most illustrious colleagues, including an *Andromeda* and a *Mars and Venus* by Titian, a *Saint George* by Parmigianino and a book of drawings by Leonardo da Vinci (quite possibly the *Atlantic Codex* now on display in the Ambrosiana). It is a great shame the entire collection was dispersed after his death.

The statues of the *Omenoni* – and the old house number 1722, which can still be seen above the entrance – are the only original elements left of this palazzo that evoked so much admiration among its contemporaries, and was praised even by the illustrious 16th-century art critic Vasari. Its uniqueness still amazes today.

Address Via degli Omenoni 3, 20121 Milan | Getting there Duomo (M1 red line,
M3 yellow line) | Tip In the nearby Piazza Meda, Arnaldo Pomodoro's *Sun* rises from
the center of a flowerbed. Created in the 1980s, the piece was moved various times
before finding its permanent home. Vigevano found it too modernistic for the
Renaissance atmosphere of its Piazza Ducale, and even the Sforza Castle rejected it.

13 _ Cascina Cuccagna
A country citadel where ideas were cultivated

Don't be misled by the name (*cascina* means "farmhouse" in Italian): this place is in the city, so you can leave your walking shoes at home. Cascina Cuccagna – a little strip of countryside, solidarity, and homespun ideas – is located in a picturesque cobblestone piazza, where the sign of an old *trattoria*, long since closed, still hangs.

It consists of more than 21,000 square feet of farmhouse, and an equal area of gardens, allotments, and courtyards, just as it was in the 18th century when it was built. Today it is one of Milan's most popular gathering spots, so rich in cultural initiatives that visitors are spoiled by the abundance of choices. It also has a very nice bistro, which has become a favorite spot for tea or aperitifs among students and locals.

There is a hostel on the upper floor, as well as a hipster-like restaurant in a large vaulted room that looks out onto the garden. Every little doorway – as in all farmhouses, there are a great many of them – is an entrance to a lab, a little shop, a new idea, a project, a show, or an artisan's studio.

First-timers can be a little disorientated by the number of things on offer, so you might want to have a look at the events listed at the entrance to the main portico or have a chat with someone at the information desk. Here, miraculously, it seems that time actually stops – and in a frenetic city like Milan, that is no small feat.

There is a free book exchange – just bring one with you and take away another. You can also sign up for a job registry, whereby you can barter with skills instead of money: if, say, you're a photographer, you can trade your services for help from a computer expert. There is something for everyone here – from yoga to origami courses, from carpentry to bike repair. And every Tuesday from 3:30pm to 8pm, there is a farmers market full of seasonal produce. It seems we're in the countryside after all!

Address Via Privata Cuccagna 2, 20135 Milan, Tel +39 0283421007, www.cuccagna.org |
Getting there Porta Romana (M 3 yellow line); Porta Romana (tram 9; bus 62, 77) |
Hours Cascina: Mon – Sun 9:30 – 1am; bar / restaurant and hostel: Tue – Sun 10 – 1am
(Tel +39 025457785, www.unpostoamilano.it) | **Tip** At Viale Monte Nero 15, there is a
bookshop called Monti in Città, which specializes in mountaineering, trekking, and the
great outdoors (Mon 3 – 7:30pm, Tue – Sat 10am – 1:30pm, 3 – 7:30pm).

14_ Cascina Monluè

General Radetzky's local tavern

"Where once there was grass, now there's a city ..." sang a nostalgic Adriano Celentano in 1966. Who knows what he would say about Cascina Monluè, a perfectly preserved old agricultural hamlet, complete with farmhouses, a church, stables, haylofts, and barns. Today it is surrounded by East Ring Road, industrial warehouses, and courier depots. Yet, just off the motorway exit, as if by magic, you will find a countryside oasis. The first thing you will notice when you arrive is the 13th-century abbey, built of redbrick, which was customary in the Lombard flatlands, where stone was scarce. A little farther on is the *cascina* itself, with its array of local characters: a man riding by on a bicycle, a woman standing at the entrance to her house, a nun giving shelter to a group of refugees in the rectory. Here everyone knows one another and is ready to assist the disoriented traveler, just as one would in any small village.

Nowadays, Monluè gets its fair share of visitors, especially on sunny days, when people come here to eat *al fresco* under the wisteria of the old inn. The restaurant is a 19th-century salon, with old paintings, cuckoo clocks, and Radetzky's proclamation from 1849 hanging on the wall in full view.

The Austrian general was a regular at the tavern, and given his well-known passion for women, he would most likely also have brought his lovers with him to one of the rooms upstairs that once accommodated visiting travelers. A painting depicts the general in a theatrical cartoon winking at a working-class girl.

The same artist dedicated a painting to Manzoni inspired by the *Promessi Sposi* (The Betrothed), depicting the Lake of Lecco with Mount Resegone in the background. Even the well-cultured author was partial to the *ossobuco risotto*, with the Milanese-style cutlet – the real one – served thick as it is only prepared here, at least according to the host.

Address Antica Trattoria Monluè, Via Monluè 75, 20138 Milan, Tel +39 027610246, www.anticatrattoriamonlue.it | **Getting there** Mecenate (tram 27) | **Tip** The Abbey of San Lorenzo, founded in 1267, was an important monastery. On one side are the old barns, which today house an institute for political refugees; on the other side is the farmhouse (currently under restoration), which the municipality uses for cultural events and exhibitions.

15__Cattelan's L.O.V.E

The rude gesture

No one could have doubted the sculpture by Maurizio Cattelan in Piazza degli Affari would arouse heated discussion. The Italian papers had a field day following its inauguration, on September 20, 2010, kicking off a fierce debate that still rages to this day.

Milan's well-to-do crowd reasoned that a little anger in response to the collapse of Lehman Brothers and the subsequent global crisis was understandable – but directing such a vulgar gesture at the Milan Stock Exchange, the heart of Italian finance … well, that was just too much. After all, we're not talking of some subtle innuendo here; the insult is crystal clear. But that's Cattelan for you – what were they expecting from an artist so famous for his irreverence?

Supposedly, there is a noble precedent explaining the significance of a hand missing four fingers, with a lonely middle finger pointing upwards: a classical statue of a Roman soldier extending his hand, missing four digits, in a salute. Even the acronym of the work's title – *L.O.V.E.*, which spells not only the English word, but also stands for the Italian words for freedom, hate, vendetta, and eternity – has sparked controversy.

Although it is referred to as "the finger" – an obvious reference to the rude gesture it brings to mind – the crippled hand is actually meant to be a caricature of the Fascist salute, and a symbol of the artist's disdain for the movement's ideals. When the 36-foot-high white Carrara marble sculpture, entitled "Against Ideologies," was unveiled at an exhibition held at Palazzo Reale, the mayor justified it by saying that it would only be a temporary installation, and others even suggested hiding it in the courtyard of a palazzo until the new museum of contemporary art could be completed. But on one point Cattelan was adamant: the sculpture is bequeathed to the city as long as it remains where it is.

Meanwhile, time goes by.

Address Piazza degli Affari, 20123 Milan | Getting there Cordusio (M1 red line); Dante/Meravigli (tram 16, 27) | Tip In Piazza Borromeo, number 12, there is an old redbrick palazzo belonging to the Borromeo family (13th century). Beyond the entrance hall, you can admire the grand courtyard, still frescoed with the geometric motifs that were in vogue at the time.

16_ Chiaravalle Abbey

The Ciribiciaccola's chant

Chiaravalle Abbey is located in the foggy hills just outside the city of Milan, among farmhouses and hay bales. The contrast between the abbey's superb architecture and the surrounding landscape of the Parco Agricolo Sud – you can buy the local delicacies in the friars' shop – is simply stunning.

The Chiaravalle Abbey was created "in the year of the Lord's favor 1135," as the plaque inside the church reads, by a group of French monks of the Order of Cîteaux, who were also responsible for drying out the local marsh. Milan owes a great deal to these monks – though the state of wild abandon in which the old canals now lie doesn't convey a great sense of gratefulness.

The atmosphere changes drastically once you set foot inside the monastery's courtyard, surrounded by an arcade, where you are suddenly captured by the sense of ancient spirituality that radiates from the walls. The interior of the church – dominated by massive brick-clad columns that sustain the central nave – is simply awe-inspiring. If you're dedicated enough to get there before 6:30am, when the chorus recites the morning prayer, or Prime, you will find yourself immersed in another time – and another dimension. The monks sit in the 17th-century walnut-colored wooden seats, beautifully inlaid by the Lombard master Carlo Garavaglia.

Beyond the transept, 16th-century paintings, known as "the Fiamminghini," – by the della Rovere brothers – depict the history of the monastic order, which was founded by Saint Bernard. The first bronze bell to be mounted according to the Ambrosian system of "balanced" bells is atop the abbey's Nolare bell tower, which is visible from a great distance. The tower's inlays and friezes are so intricately decorated that the locals nicknamed it *Ciribiciaccola* (literally "clever contraption") – a word in ancient Lombard dialect used to describe a complex wheel-based device.

Address Via Sant'Arialdo 102, 20139 Milan, Tel +39 0257403404 | Getting there
Corvetto (M3 yellow line; bus 77) | Hours Tue–Sat 9am–noon/2:30–5:30pm,
Sun 2:30–5:30pm (free guided tours on Sundays until 4pm) | Tip At Via San Dionigi
6 you can find the statue of Christ the Redeemer, confidentially called "El Signurun de
Milan" (*Signurun* means "Jesus" in Milanese dialect), placed there to bless the pilgrims
who entered the city after stopping at the abbey.

17__Cimitero Monumentale

A walk among Milan's most renowned families

You can while away the hours in the neoclassical gardens of the Cimitero Monumentale (Monumental Cemetery) in the company of some very illustrious figures: women in mourning, winged cherubs, musicians, sphinxes, and convivial tables, like the one in *Last Supper* by Giannino Castiglioni, executed in bronze and stone for the tomb of the Campari family, which the Milanese have jokingly nicknamed *L'ultimo aperitivo* ("the last aperitif").

The Cimitero Monumentale was designed in 1866 by the prominent architect Carlo Maciachini (1818–1899) to celebrate the city's independence from foreign rule. While it is open to all living people, it's a lot more discerning when it comes to the dead, for whom access is conditional upon having a prodigious curriculum vitae, as well as some other essential requisites, which are minutely examined by a strict selection committee. You could say that the entire history of Milan, from the Risorgimento onward, is squeezed into these sixty-plus acres of marble and cypress trees.

All the top families are here: Frette, Belloni, Marelli, Zambeletti, Treccani, Bonelli, Fumagalli, Morandi, Biraghi, Visconi, Riva, Campari, Falck, etc. It's almost a city within the city, centered around the Famedio, the pantheon of VIPs that houses the tomb of the poet Alessandro Manzoni, flanked by the monuments to Carlo Cattaneo and Giuseppe Verdi. One can also read the epitaphs of the illustrious Salvatore Quasimodo and Francesco Hayez.

The eclectic architecture shifts freely from one style to another, but the most beautiful tombs are to be found outside the Famedio, among the flowerbeds edged by temples, Egyptian pyramids, and group sculptures.

This is truly an open-air museum, featuring the works of famous artists such as Lucio Fontana, Bruno Munari, Aldo Pomodoro, Medardo Rosso, Luca Beltrami, and Giacomo Manzù.

Address Piazzale Cimitero Monumentale, 20154 Milan | Getting there Monumentale (M5 lilac line); Garibaldi (M2 green line); Monumentale (tram 12, 14; bus 37) | Hours Tue–Sun 8am–6pm | Tip Giuseppe Verdi's real tomb is in Piazza Michelangelo Buonarroti, in the crypt of the home for retired musicians, which the composer founded in 1899.

18_ CityLife
The starchitect's fair

For some time now Milan has been invaded by "starchitects." It has become quite the trend – and just as well. After years of partying and bacchanalian feasts, mirrored in the catchy slogan *Milano da bere* ("Drinkin' Milan"), the city eventually got a wake-up call.

The alarm bell was a reminder of the glorious past of the Lombard capital as a leader in industry and innovation – attested to by its hosting of the 1906 World Expo. Everyone wanted a spot in one of the pavilions – designed by the best architects of the day and temporarily placed in the estate of the Sforza Castle, which was then renamed Parco Sempione (Simplon Park), to celebrate the inauguration of the Alpine Simplon Tunnel.

What a shame that the designs of papier-mâché and plaster were all dismantled – except for the Civic Aquarium and the Torre Branca (Branca Tower), which are still located in the park. As for Portello, the neighborhood that once hosted the Fiera Campionaria (Trade Fair) and is today at the center of Milan's "architectural renaissance," we can consider its transformation to be permanent – so long as its new string of skyscrapers doesn't collapse, that is.

CityLife, Milan's new residential and financial hub, is centered around the three twisting towers of Arata Isozaki, Zaha Hadid, and Daniel Libeskind. These have significantly altered the emotional skyline that the Milanese have loved for centuries, with the Monte Rosa as its backdrop.

On closer inspection, the new MiCo convention center is reminiscent of the papier-mâché buildings of 1906, with its crumpled look and seemingly provisional panels, which are actually made of anodized aluminum. They call it the "Comet" because it glistens day and night, thanks to the LEDs inserted in its structure. The architect Mario Bellini managed to achieve an extraordinary light display, resulting in a voluminous silver tail 650 feet high.

TORRE LIBESKIND

metri 150

RIQUALIFICAZIONE
DELL'EX PADIGLIONE

Address MiCo Centro Congressi. Entrances: Gate 2 Viale Eginardo and Gate 17 Piazzale Carlo Magno, 20149 Milan, www.micomilano.it | **Getting there** Amendola (M1 red line); Eginardo/Colleoni, Gate 2 and Colleoni/Gattamelata, Gate 17 (bus 78); Piazza VI Febbraio, Gate 17 (tram 27) | **Hours** Tue–Sun 8am–6pm | **Tip** In front of Gate 17, though the entrance is at Via Arona 19, is the Vigorelli Velodrome, the "magical" racetrack inaugurated in 1935. Entirely covered with wooden floorboards, it is unique in the world and has hosted several cycling championships.

19_ The Civic Aquarium

The sea world's Art Nouveau pavilion

Compared to the dazzling underwater scenes featured at most modern Italian aquariums – such as the one in Genoa – Milan's old pavilion, built for the 1906 World Exposition, evokes a comforting sense of intimacy. The largest tank is very modest in size compared to that of more contemporary aquariums, though a three-year-long restoration project, undertaken in 2003, brought the institute's system up to current standards, enabling it to continue its educational vocation, which the Milanese are very committed to, as demonstrated by the school groups that fill the aquarium year-round.

It is the third oldest aquarium in Europe, and thus should be appreciated more as an archaeological site than anything else. Yet the Civic Aquarium's more modern didactic is not to be dismissed: it offers a reproduction of the various Italian aquatic ecosystems, from the Alpine torrent to the Mediterranean Sea, from Lake Como to the River Po's embankment. It also includes a ring-shaped circuit – where the visitor can choose to follow the tide or "swim" against it like a salmon – as well as the sunken wreck of an oil tanker.

But what sets this building apart from others is its unique Viennese Art Nouveau style. It is the only pavilion from the old Expo to remain standing to this day. Its architect, Sebastiano Locati, knew from the start that the place was destined to become an aquarium – hence his decision to use water-themed ornamentation on the facades in bas-relief.

Today the building is probably best appreciated from the outside: it is worth taking a stroll around it to admire the fish, octopuses, and crustaceans that swirl around the friezes and pilasters. There is something unique about this cement zoo surrounded by the trees of Sempione Park. At the entrance, don't forget to check out the fountain of Poseidon with a hippopotamus head below it that spouts water from its mouth.

Address Viale Gerolamo Gadio 2, 20121 Milan, Tel +39 0288445392,
www.acquariocivicomilano.eu | Getting there Lanza (M 2 green line; tram 2, 12, 14;
bus 57, 61) | Hours Tue–Sun 9am–1pm/2–5:30pm | Tip Inside the park, close to the
arena, is the "Rotten Water Fountain," today in a state of abandon. Its waters, rich in
manganese and sulphur, were considered by the Milanese to have miraculous healing
properties.

20 Conca dell'Incoronata

When Brera was a little Venice

The great wooden gates that once blocked the flow of water in Milan's canals were designed by Leonardo da Vinci. His drawings of the gates were published in the famous *Atlantic Codex*, which can be admired at the Biblioteca Ambrosiana. These weather-worn, powerful sluices, with their gates still intact, half open, can be seen at the end of Via San Marco, ready to hold back water that is no longer there.

Restored in 1996, and then subsequently neglected again, today the sluices act as a refuge for stray cats and a rubbish dump for windswept litter, which gathers under the brick sentry box and the bridge, the only one built in *ceppo d'Adda* stone. It was a crucial thoroughfare connecting the town built around the Navigli to the Martesana, the canal that linked Milan to the Adda River, extending well beyond the Spanish Walls (built by the city's Spanish rulers in the 16th century). Originally at the height of the "Tombon de San Marc," the site was later moved about 300 feet.

This is where duty was paid on goods and people entering the city, which is why the place came to be known as Ponte delle Gabelle ("Gabelle" after the unpopular salt tax of the same name). Its current name, Conca dell'Inconorata, refers to the 14th-century church of Santa Maria Incoronata. The old-city atmosphere of the place, so rare to find these days, is accentuated by the picturesque *piazzetta*, where a typical palazzo – once used as a warehouse to store goods that were loaded and unloaded in the small port – has been transformed into the Carlsberg beer house. It is worth taking a walk downstairs in the building where you can see the old vaulted red-brick ceilings, and, hanging on the wall, pictures of a time when water still flowed through the Naviglio. The lively and trendy district of Brera is distracting, though, and those who frequent it don't often come this far down.

Address At the end of Via San Marco, at number 45, 20121 Milan | Getting there
Transit Moscova (M 2 green line); Principessa Clotilde (bus 43); Pontaccio (bus 61) |
Tip At Via San Marco 20 is Brera's most famous restaurant, the legendary El Tombon
de San Marc, which takes its name from the old port where the Martesana canal
connected to the internal circuit of the Navigli.

21 Corso Como 10

The gallery owner's apartment building

Fashionable, international, and – let's say it – a little snobby. Corso Como 10 is the city space of gallery owner Carla Sozzani: a concept-store, which, at the end of the 1980s when it was created, was considered very innovative, and is still trendy today among soccer players, models, and celebrities of all types, also thanks to its proximity to the famous Hollywood disco.

There is a restaurant, a bar, and an art bookshop, as well as an off-beat bazaar of objects and curiosities from all over the world. The place really strives to be unconventional, though it is less and less so, partly as a result of the skyscrapers that have completely transformed the neighborhood.

The old apartment-block atmosphere has been tastefully re-interpreted in a modern key. There's a comfortable sitting room – crowded, welcoming, expensive – where you can relax on one of the colored sofas. The entrance, an ivy-framed doorway, is discreet. Entering the courtyard, it is easy to trip over the many plants and various vases scattered around in apparent disarray. But a closer look reveals a painstaking attention to detail. People come here for "happy hour," but once they gather at the outside tables, they want to stay all night.

Take time to explore all the different spaces of this original-period housing block, from the colored resin floors, where shells and other marine fragments have been trapped, to the sculptures. On the floor above you will find a library and a photographic gallery – the true passion of the *signora*.

The cherry on top is the roof terrace (when it is open), which few people know about: packed with plants, it is just like any old terrace, except it offers an unusual and charming view of the skyline of Piazza Gae Aulenti, with Unicredit's skyscraper in the background, towering over the defiant apartment buildings of a Milan long gone.

Address Corso Como 10, 20154 Milan | Getting there Porta Garibaldi (M2 green line) | Hours Mon–Sun 10:30am–7:30pm (Thu and Sat open till 9pm); bar and restaurant 11am–1am | Tip At Corso Como 15 is the Hollywood disco, famous for its celebrity regulars from the world of soccer, television, and fashion. Just browse the website to get a taste of its clientele (www.discotecahollywood.it).

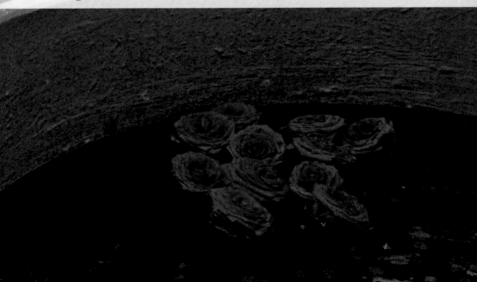

22 Corso di Porta Ticinese

The walls are talking

You'll know you have reached Corso di Porta Ticinese in Carrobbio when the posh characteristics of the city – the beautiful buildings, clean streets, and world-class shop windows – are nowhere to be found. In the *Promessi Sposi* (*The Betrothed*), Manzoni described this as "one of the most desolate parts of Milan."

If you look closely, at the entrance you will note a small blue sign with the words *Il bla bla uccide* ("blah blah kills"). As you continue along the left side of the street toward the *porta* (gate), with its ancient tower, the messages become more frequent.

Most people hardly notice them, but the half-torn paper leaflets glued to the walls between the shops and the doorways are not advertisements; they are the angry, lyrical, ironic, and sometimes romantic fragments of a metropolitan poem: "… my voice rises over the buildings, it bursts forth but in vain, I try to control my trembling hands by smoking … my words are suffocated even before they are thoughts." They are collectively signed by the "Movimento per L'Emancipazione della Poesia" (Movement for the Emancipation of Poetry). This is serious stuff.

Somewhat more lighthearted is the gold-framed collage of lyrics and comics depicting a young man in front of a TV: "The government has some great programs, but the problem is the license." Similar puns and gags are directed at the austerity policies of recent years.

Farther on, near Saint Lawrence's columns, the leaflets become monumental graffiti or hacked blackboards, just as the one belonging to the poor Japanese restaurant whose sushi menu is almost entirely covered by chalk phrases like the one advertising, "bags under your eyes designed by a well-known fashion designer."

The Milanese have renamed this place Colonne ("columns"). And as a young girl has scribbled on the wall, "You can't look at the new day with yesterday's eyes."

Address Corso di Porta Ticinese, 20123 Milan | Getting there Ticinese (bus 94, 163); Correnti (tram 2, 14) | Hours Thu–Sun 6–10:30pm; visits can be arranged at other times by calling the number +39 3317570256 between 9am and 1pm (www.casadelleartiste.it) | Tip At Via Magolfa 32 is the Museo Casa delle Arti, dedicated to the poet Alda Merini, who lived on the Navigli. You can view a section of the famous "wall of angels," on which the artist wrote fragments of intense poetry defined by her experience in an asylum.

23__ The Crying Madonna

In the courtyard of the old leper colony

Milan has its very own weeping Madonna. Not the famous Madonnina, but the Virgin and Child painted by a monk from Mount Athos and donated to the Russian Orthodox congregation of the Church of Saint Nicholas. A sign on the street indicates the side entrance, which might otherwise go unnoticed. From there, you enter a courtyard immersed in vegetation – there are so many vases and plants scattered around that you can hardly move, and the space is made even more cramped by the dozens of sacred icons, crucifixes, candlesticks, and water pitchers that fill the portico in front of the chapels.

This tiny hybrid between a garden and a courtyard is a veritable oasis of peace and serenity. While sitting on a bench under the loggia, you can sometimes hear, wafting from the first chapel, the soft, plaintive singing of foreign women praying in their own language. Protected under a red velvet canopy, the Virgin and Child receive their guests. And occasionally she weeps, maybe in response to the pain of those who visit: Christians escaping persecution in the Middle East, Eritreans, Russians, Moldavians, and Romanians. The baby Jesus weeps as well. It appears to be a type of vegetable oil that emanates a perfumed essence and leaves no trace on the painting. The phenomenon was first witnessed in the spring of 2010, and is now observed on a regular basis, each time drawing a steady crowd of pilgrims. Legend has it that after visiting the Virgin Mary, a woman was cured of cancer, while another one, apparently unable to have children, gave birth to a healthy boy.

The Metropolitan bishop Evloghios, an 80-year-old man sporting a long white beard, confirms that the mystery "cannot be humanly explained." But believe it or not, one thing is certain: nestled in the noisy district between Corso Buenos Aires and the central station, this welcoming courtyard is a miracle unto itself.

Address Chiesa Ortodossa Russa San Nicola, Via San Gregorio 5, 20124 Milan |
Getting there Lima (M 1 red line); Settembrini (tram 1, 5); Tunisia (tram 1, 5) | Tip
At number 20 Corso Buenos Aires – the avenue of shops built in the 19th century
after the demolition of the leper colony of the Lazzaretto – is the historic Ambrosiano
coffee shop, a small but delightful bar offering a wide variety of coffees (Mon – Sun
7am – 7:30pm).

24_ The Devil's Column

The mysteries of the Basilica of Saint Ambrogio

There had to be a story behind it, given that it is the only marble column outside the consecrated area, right in front of Milan's most revered basilica (after the Duomo, that is) dedicated to the city's patron saint, Saint Ambrogio. Corinthian in style, it dates back to the 2nd century. It is hardly noticeable to passersby, since it is overshadowed by the beauty of the four-sided portico of the basilica. Its significance, however, should not be underestimated: this column is nothing less than a totem against evil.

Legend has it that the saint defeated the devil incarnate here. Saint Ambrogio was an important spiritual figure during the first centuries of the Christian era, and his followers firmly believed that a real battle took place here, during which Satan unwittingly rammed the column with his horns, punching two holes into it, which can be seen in the lower part. Some say you can still smell sulphur in the air. There might well be some truth in the legend, considering that the area is a cemetery for Christian martyrs. Who knows what went on here after sunset once upon a time – what with ghosts, prejudices, and the power of suggestion.

There was certainly something special about this place if, during the Middle Ages future kings would come here to embrace the column of the basilica before being crowned and pledging allegiance to the Pope. Its sister column, equally mysterious, is made of porphyry and can be found inside the nave of the church. It is easily recognizable because it acts as a pedestal for a bronze serpent that, according to legend, was forged in the desert by Moses himself.

The Milanese attribute to it magical powers, saying it is capable of curing reptile bites. Not even Saint Ambrogio was able to completely dispel pagan beliefs!

Oh, and don't forget: they say that it's good luck to put your fingers through the holes.

Address Piazza Sant'Ambrogio 15, 20123 Milan | Getting there Sant'Ambrogio (M 2 green line | Hours Mon–Sat 7:30am–12:30pm/2:30–7pm, Sun and holidays 7:30am–1pm/3:20–5pm | Tip In the nearby Università Cattolica, there is free access to the famous Bramante cloisters, commissioned by Ludovico il Moro, which used to seat the old monastery of Saint Ambrogio, suppressed by Napoleon in 1799.

25 Dialogo nel Buio

Seeing without looking

A walk in the dark here will allow you to discover the incredible world of the visually impaired – full of life, sounds, smells, and tactile experiences. As you stumble like a child who is learning to walk, the most familiar places – a garden lawn, a city street, a public park – will suddenly "appear" alien and mysterious. But as you grope your way through the darkness, stepping on people's toes and clumsily maneuvering with your stick, constantly bumping into the others and laughing with embarrassment, the initial sense of unease slowly dissipates. Everyone is a friend here, maybe because they've never seen each other before – and can't even see each other now.

The blind young woman who acts as a guide plays her trump card, putting your perceptions to the test by asking you to perform various tasks: touch the coarse hair of a horse, smell the perfume of a fruit, climb into a boat (but pay attention to the steps: the water is still there even if you can't see it!). Amid the chaos of the city, the sound of car horns and rattling trams hint at threats and dangers lurking in all directions. It can be unsettling, but then, it's supposed to be. (Besides, you're in a safe environment.)

Slowly the darkness reveals itself: in fact, it is not an "empty void" but rather a place full of objects, people, and emotional encounters. Scents you wouldn't normally notice become recognizable, such as grass, while the smoothness or roughness of bark is what allows you to distinguish a pine tree from a birch.

As you move along a wall, a sudden draft makes you aware of an open door. You have not entered a new world, you are simply rediscovering a familiar one through different senses. By the time you reach the Cafènoir, any fear of the darkness has been exorcised, and all that is left to do is to pay the bill.

Have you ever noticed that a 50-cent piece is larger than a euro coin?

Address Istituto dei Ciechi, Via Vivaio 7, 20122 Milan, Tel +39 0276394478, www.dialogonelbuio.org | Getting there Palestro and San Babila (M1 red line); Monforte/Donizetti (bus 54, 61) | Hours Guided tours, winter: Tue and Wed 9:45am–4pm, Thu and Fri 9:45am–4pm/6:30–8:30pm, Sat 2:15–9pm, Sun 11:15am–6:15pm; summer: Tue and Wed 2:30–6:30pm, Thu and Fri 2:30–8:30pm | Tip The Cafénoir, located inside the institute, provides the unique experience of an aperitif in total darkness, while listening to live music (Thu–Sat from 7pm).

26 — Eataly

Shopping at the theater

Eataly, in no small part thanks to its catchy brand name, has become in just a few years a point of reference in the field of gastronomic excellence. It also symbolizes a different approach to food shopping, one that endorses small producers. From the countryside straight to the counter, from the flour mill straight to the oven: the idea is to promote a way of eating that is both healthy and ethical, guided by principles of sustainability, responsibility, and sharing.

If you think this is yet another case of "all talk no action," head over to this "supermarket" in Piazza XXV Aprile and have a walk through the aisles; you'll see that this is the real deal. The products are divided along thematic and regional lines. Take the sweets section, for example: Domori cocoa beans, Baratti and Milano hazelnut cream, spreadable pistachio from Bronte, not to mention the nougat of the Antica Torroneria Piemontese. Should you fancy a coffee, there's even a cafe.

Upstairs is the charcuterie section, which Lombardy is famous for. Good luck resisting the smells inviting you to the tasting tables. There's an incredible selection of cheeses as well, beginning with the giant tub filled with über-fresh mozzarellas from Puglia. Then there is all the rest, from the balsamic vinegar of Modena to the lard of Colonnata and the truffles of Alba. There is a veritable feast for the palate here and you can take it home or eat it on the spot.

The location – a former theater – is also impeccable. Where once there was the foyer, stalls, and balcony, there are now three floors of shelves full of PGI (Protected Geographical Indication) products. All this surrounds a suspended stage in the center of the food hall, a memorial to the historic theater, on which musicians take turns entertaining the shoppers.

Even the selection of live concerts is PGI, though the volume of the loudspeakers is at times a tad excessive.

Address Piazza 25 XXV 10, 20121 Milan, Tel +39 0249497301, www.eataly.it |
Getting there Moscova and Garibaldi (M 2 green line); Gioia / Garibaldi (bus 37) |
Hours Mon – Sun 10am – midnight | **Tip** In the basement of Via Giuseppe Marcora
8 there is a flea market called *tra noi e voi* ("between us"), where anyone can buy or sell
(closed Tuesdays, www.almercatinotranoievoi.com).

27 __ Erba Brusca

A vegetable garden on the table

This whole area, irrigated by the waters of the Naviglio Pavese, was once all countryside, and to some extent it still is. The cycling path, which goes as far as Pavia, winds its way through a landscape of flatlands and farmsteads. On Sundays it teems with cyclists.

Erba Brusca has today replaced the old out-of-the-way tavern, while the bowling green has become a vegetable and aromatic herb garden. The place has changed a lot since it was taken over in 2011 by Danilo Ingannamorte and Alice Delcourt, whose expertise is backed by the prestigious Ratanà restaurant.

"Those who know us, know what to expect, without the need to resort to flashy signs," says Danilo. The decent-sized vegetable garden also includes sorrel, a weed that is usually chucked away by farmers, but is a particular favorite of Alice's for its wild aroma. It gives her cooking that hint of acidity, especially in one of her signature dishes: spaghetti with clams, black truffle, and sorrel.

They are quite a duo: he is a sommelier; she is an internationally trained chef with the skill of an alchemist when it comes to balancing vegetables. The tables outside are set with recycled brown paper, just as they used to be in the old taverns, but the dishes are top class, served with rural simplicity as a tribute to their true value. Speaking of which, it is enough to watch the chef at work in her huge open-plan kitchen to know that she is the real deal. Resistance is futile; just relax and let Alice work her magic. The menu gives you only a price, as is the latest trend with the new generation of Parisian bistros: 30 euros for a four-course meal, take it or leave it, and "Enjoy!"

A final footnote: for an additional 22 euros you can get the selection of "blind wines," six different tastings chosen by Danilo. It's the best way to try an unusual wine, perhaps a French *cru*, and to unwind in style.

Address Alzaia Naviglio Pavese 286, 20142 Milan, Tel +39 0287380711,
www.erbabrusca.it | Getting there Abbiategrasso (M2 green line + a mile on foot);
Chiesa Rossa / Conca Fallata (bus 79) | Hours Wed – Sun lunch and dinner (Wed
evening live jazz) | Tip Davide Longoni is the baker and owner of Panificio Davide
Longoni, Via Tiraboschi 19, which is open also on Sunday mornings. Needless to say,
all the flour is organic (www.panificiodavidelongoni.com).

28___The Fake Hillock

Where athletes train and the righteous are remembered

This strange city park, with its conical formation reminiscent of the Tower of Babel, rose out of the ruins of World War II. The rubble of the buildings that collapsed under the bombing raids of 1943 and 1944 had to be put somewhere, and so, during the postwar reconstruction period, the 160-foot-high Monte Stella project was conceived.

An extraordinary view of the Alps awaits you at the top, but you have to get there, and this requires considerable stamina. Thanks to the terrain's unevenness, it has become a common training ground for athletes, race walkers, runners, and cyclists. Paths and walkways sinuously curl around it, intersecting to create endless possibilities of routes, although the more intrepid bikers favor the steep downhill slopes and shortcuts. Planted 50 years ago, the trees – among them maple, hackberry, elm, glades of birch, plane, cedar, and horse chestnut – have grown to create an environment that is cool and welcoming in the summer.

The funny thing is that in the winter a sprinkling of snow is enough for the *montagnetta* – as the Milanese affectionately call it – to fill up with sleds, snowboards, and skiers. It is incredible that such a small hill, dwarfed by the Alps, should become such a playground.

In 2003, seventy-four acres were dedicated to those who devoted their lives to benefitting humanity; thus the Giardino dei Giusti (Garden of the Righteous) was born. For each person honored a tree has been planted: among them Peter Kuciukian, a surgeon and writer who was awarded the City of Milan's Golden Ambrogino; the Norwegian explorer Fridtjof Nansen, winner of the 1922 Nobel Peace Prize; Samir Kassir, the Lebanese politician assassinated in 2005; and Russian journalist Anna Politkovskaya, who denounced the massacre of Chechen civilians and then was herself murdered in 2006. From seeds like these, it is only natural that strong trees should blossom.

Address There are four entrances: Via Cimabue (for the Giardino dei Giusti), Sant'Elia, Via Enrico Terzaghi, and Via Isernia, 20148 Milan | **Getting there** QT 8 (M 1 red line); Santa Maria Nascente (bus 68); Croce/ Sant'Elia (bus 40, 69) | **Tip** At Via Paolo Uccello 19 is Villa Fossati, known as the "sad villa," where in June of 1944 the infamous Koch gang set themselves up. Here the Nazis tortured political prisoners. The Fossati family, not wishing to return to live here, donated it to a religious institution that still resides in it.

29 The Fashion District
Among revolutionaries and models off the catwalk

Walking down Via Della Spiga means sharing the pavement with long-legged models fresh from a photo shoot, Eastern European oligarchs with their wives swathed in leopard prints, and mysterious veiled dames (and their male counterparts). Prada, Moschino, Vogue, Valentino, Armani: they're all here, in their over-the-top extravaganza and brightly lit windows.

The elegant ladies, bless them, enter with a smile and exit with an even bigger smile, their bags of haute couture purchases on their arms: stiletto shoes, crocodile and snakeskin handbags, and smoldering figure-hugging dresses made of tulle and silk.

And to think that the high-fashion district (known as the golden rectangle of fashion), between Montenapoleone and Via Senato – where the Naviglio still flowed until the 1930s – used to be home to small merchants, artisans' workshops, taverns, middle-class houses, communal bathhouses, stables, and courtyards for the carriages.

During the Risorgimento, it was a revolutionary hotbed: Francesco Restelli, who later became a senator of the Kingdom of Italy, lived at number 17 on Via Della Spiga; in Palazzo Garzanti (at number 30) Cesare Correnti laid down the 1848 manifesto that kick-started the Five Days revolt against Austrian occupation; and at the Merlo cafe, revolutionaries engaged in lively debates about the new forms of alienation produced by the industrial revolution.

Some of the old shops – the grocer nicknamed Garibaldi, the wine shop with hard-boiled eggs on the counter, the button shop – held out until the 1950s, but eventually closed. However, already in 1863 the jeweler Annibale Cusi was designing diamond chokers for Her Majesty the Queen of the Kingdom of Italy. His first shop was on Via Napoleone, before he moved to Via Clerici.

And to think: many of the 17th-century *palazzi* in this district were once home to convents!

Address Via della Spiga – Via Montenapoleone, 20121 Milan | **Getting there**
San Babila (M1 red line), Montenapoleone (M3 yellow line); Senato (bus 61, 94);
Manzoni (tram 1) | **Tip** Cusi, owner of the eponymous jewelry shop founded
in 1886, won first prize at the 1906 Expo for his "Mary Stuart" choker, featuring
15,000 diamonds. The shop relocated to Via Clerici 1, which today houses the Caffè
Victoria; if you look up, you can see the commemoration plaque on the side of
Via Porrone. The jewelry shop is still run by the Cusi family and is now at Corso
Monforte 23 (San Babila).

30 _ Fiera di Sinigaglia

A flea market filled with treasures

Located in the Porta Genova District, the Fiera di Sinigaglia is the most loved and busiest flea market in Milan, though it has been drastically reduced in size, much to the fury of the locals. The stall owners marched on town hall, local newspapers screamed bloody murder, but all to no avail: the fate of this historic market – which the *Corriere della Sera* in 1906 described as a place "where you can find anything, even something beautiful, a work of art maybe, but especially all those things that have an air of being utterly useless" – was sealed.

This market dates back to the 19th century, when groups of rag-and-bone men would meet at the intersection of the Naviglio Grande and the Darsena, a former commercial port, and trade merchandise with the poor. Today, the 150 stalls have been exiled to the former parking lot behind the Porta Genova station, and if you don't know Milan, you might be wary of going inside, given its run-down and slum-like appearance. But looks can be deceiving.

Every weekend, entire cellars are emptied into the market's stalls for sale. On Saturday mornings you can discover little gems among the bric-a-brac, or with a few euros buy a bicycle to ride around the city. All in all, you can strike some good deals at the Sinigaglia Fair – as you can at Milan's other historic flea market, the Bonola, which is open on Sundays.

Of course, if a beautiful setting is what is most important to you, there is still the Mercatone dell'Antiquariato, which is held on the last Sunday of the month on the banks of the Naviglio Grande. It palpitates with appointments, exchanges, bargains, and bartering – a colorful and crowded open-air emporium. There are 400 stalls of vintage objects, antique furniture, books, vinyl records, and every kind of antique you can imagine. And for this monthly Sunday occasion, all the shops and bars on the Naviglio remain open.

Address Alzaia Naviglio Grande (at Valenza), 20154 Milan | Getting there Porta Genova (M2 green line); Porta Genova (tram 2, 9); Valenza (bus 47, 74) | Hours Fiera di Sinigaglia, Sat 8am–6pm; Mercato di Bonola, Sun 7am–2pm; Mercatone dell'Antiquariato (Naviglio Grande) last Sunday of the month 9am–6pm (except July) | Tip Nipper (Ripa di Porta Ticinese 69) is an antique shop specializing in period radios, which they both sell and expertly restore (www.nipper.it).

31 Fondazione Pirelli
A Formula One archive

Today it is known mainly for the tires mounted on Ferrari racing cars, but back in the day, Pirelli made much more than just tires, as evidenced in this archive: from the latex swimsuit worn by Marilyn Monroe to raincoats; from the linoleum flooring found in gyms to stiletto heels; from the diving mask worn by 007 – and mentioned by Ian Fleming in *Octopussy* – to foam-rubber sofas. It's a long journey that began in 1872 and spanned the 20th century, especially in Milan. Its symbol *par excellence* is the Pirellone, once the highest skyscraper in Europe. It was built between 1956 and 1960 on the ruins of the original factory, which was destroyed in the war, and housed the company's management offices, until they were relocated to the Bicocca neighborhood.

Pirelli has always stood out from the crowd, with its strong and racy ads – not easy in prudish and Catholic Italy. How to forget its risqué calendars, which were a guaranteed feature in every garage and truck cab the country? The archive's showroom is also like no other: there are TV ads from the 1960s projected on the floor, and an enormous interactive board to play with. An illuminated chessboard chronicles the years of economic boom, the film stars, the Formula One races, and the construction of Milan's metro. Every six months the theme changes; there's no lack of material, after all.

You can view documentaries from 1912, or the 1966 film by Hugh Hudson in which a Pirelli truck pursues a GT driven by a beautiful woman. Two copies remain of the film: one here and one at the MoMA in New York City.

Downstairs are the archive vaults, where the *sancta sanctorum* relics – the holiest of the holiest – are kept, including 200 original sketches by the likes of Ugo Mulas, Bruno Munari, Renato Guttuso, and Jean Grignani, as well as publicity campaigns dating back to the 1920s that have fueled the imaginations of millions of Italians.

Address Viale Sarca 222, 20126 Milan, Tel +39 0264423971, www.fondazionepirelli.org |
Getting there Ponale (M5 lilac line); Sarca/San Glicerio-Chiese (bus 728) | Hours
Mon–Fri 10am–5pm (bookings only) | Tip Through the trees where Viale Sarca
crosses Via Pirelli, you can see the lovely 15th-century farmhouse called Bicocca degli
Arcimboldi, from which the district gets its name.

32 Fonderia Napoleonica Eugenia

A former bronze foundry

The old Fonderia Eugenia (Eugenia Foundry) is the fruit of an expropriation. In 1806, Napoleon, who had little regard for the property of the Church, confiscated several buildings from the adjoining Santa Maria Alla Fontana Church. The gate leading into the yard is closed. This is private property, so you can only take a peek if you have booked a visit. The foundry's redbrick buildings overlooking the yard have today been turned into offices. It is a delightful place, unknown to most people despite its illustrious history.

This is where the giant *sestiga* on the top of the Arco Della Pace was forged. In the second half of the 19th century, the workshop was taken over by the Barigozzi brothers, specialist bell makers, as can be seen from the old photographs exhibited on the first floor. At the time it was common for craftsmen not to have a fixed address but to travel as and when required.

Today, entering the room where the bronze was cast, it seems as if the bricks are still giving off heat, mingling with the sweat of the workers and the acrid odor of the metal – a combination of muscle power, manual dexterity, and expertise that came together to create the special melodious quality of the bells. To get a feel for the past, head over to the museum, where the entire creative process is explained from start to finish. You can also take a look at the molds for the bells, as well as the panels in terra-cotta and chalk depicting angels and holy scenes that were used to decorate them. Their strokes still resound in the churches of many small Catholic communities across Africa, Asia, and Latin America, but also in the campanile of San Marco in Venice and Santa Maria del Fiore in Florence. The Barigozzi descendants are proud of their heritage and are here to preserve its memory.

Address Via Genova Thaon di Revel 21, 2015 Milan, Tel +39 3930552272,
www.fonderianapoleonica.it | Getting there Zara (M 3 yellow line); Stelvio / Farini
(bus 90, 92) | Hours Advance booking is required (museo@fonderianapoleonica.it),
except on special occasions (consult the website) | Tip In the middle of Piazza Duomo
is the equestrian monument dedicated to Victor Emmanuel II, forged in the studio of
the Barigozzi brothers in 1896.

33 _Galleria Campari

A fizzy message

Even fizzier than the actual drink is the marketing campaign associated with the now famous Campari bottle, designed by Fortunato Depero in 1928 and produced by Campari in 1932. The bottle tells a story of glamor and traditions that began 150 years ago. The avant-garde lettering of the Campari logo, designed by Bruno Munari, lined the stations of the red line metro on the day of its opening, in 1964.

Today, in the *galleria* in Sesto San Govanni, you can marvel at dozens of original posters designed by the most creative "ad men" of the time. The two-story red-draped gallery is seductive in its description of the drinking habits of the new century. It is located in the old brick factory of 1904, which has been incorporated into a new building designed by the architect Mario Botta. Here, the posters and interactive screens chronicle the transformation of the brand over the years: from Adolf Hohenstein's mustached men – a cross between realism and Art Nouveau – to the visionary graphics of Depero, who was known to enjoy his cordial or bitter in the company of his Futurist friends Marinetti and Bocconi in the bar of the Galleria Vittorio Emanuele, founded by Gaspare Campari in 1867.

Depero is also the man behind the Cubist-like ad featuring the geometric figure with the slogan "*distrattamente mise il bitter campari in testa*" (literally, "he distractedly put the bitter campari on his head") – an ad way ahead of its time, as ironic and unpredictable as the Futurist movement that rallied around the magazine *Parole in libertà* ("free-wheeling words").

The Campari company embraced this new form of communication. It hired the best illustrators available and sought access to the most exclusive get-togethers in Milan, which were getting more and more worldly by the day, especially given that many women were beginning to indulge their thirst for fun.

Address Viale Antonio Gramsci 161, 20099 Sesto San Giovanni (MI),
Tel +39 0262251, www.campari.com | Getting there Sesto Rondò (M 1 red line) |
Hours Tue, Thu, and Fri with guided tours at 2pm, 3:30pm, and 5pm; first Saturday
 of the month at 10am, 11:30am, 2pm, 3:30pm, and 5pm (it is possible to book
foreign-language tours). | Tip The old Campari villa, on the north side of the park,
is today an elegant restaurant with covered outdoor seating. On occasions, themed
events are held here, such as "Futurist" dinners (Via Davide Campari 23,
Tel +39 0222471108, www.villacampariristorante.it).

34_ Gallerie d'Italia

In the vaults of the bank

In the historic headquarters of the Banca Commerciale, behind the brass counters, there are paintings by Afro, Vedova, Capogrossi, Guttuso, and Melotti – some of the best Italian painters of the postwar period. The bank, now part of the Intesa Sanpaolo Group, acquired the works over the years to adorn its foreign branches – a sort of modern-day patronage.

Until recently the paintings were not viewable by the Italian public, since they were confined to the bank's various overseas offices, where they were exhibited with pride. But today the collection is preserved in three prestigious palazzi, one of which is in Piazza della Scala, in Milan. And so the Gallerie d'Italia (Italian Galleries) project was conceived. In an Art Nouveau setting of glass, columns, and priceless marble, pop meets conceptual art meets transavantgarde ("beyond the avant-garde") meets "poor art."

But the true secret is in the basement, in the former vault of the Banca Commerciale. Down the red velvet-carpeted staircase leading to the once gold- and jewel-filled crypt, is a massive steel door, behind which is the safe where the better-off Milanese once entrusted their treasures. Today, those treasures have been replaced by 500 works of art that there was no room to house on the floor above. But don't for a moment think that they are hidden here because they are less worthy – unless you consider a late Picasso or a black "cretto" by Burri, mounted on sliding grills where the safe-deposit boxes were once stored, of little consequence.

The vault is open to the public once a month. It is difficult to decide which is better: to listen to the guide talking about Balla, Carrà, and Sironi, or to admire the ionic columns and ironwork of the room, into which the Milanese noblewomen would descend to retrieve their diamond necklaces before heading off to La Scala to hear Maria Callas.

Address Piazza della Scala 6, 20121 Milan, Tel +39 800167619,
www.gallerieditalia.com | **Getting there** Duomo (M 1 red line and M 3 yellow line);
Manzoni (tram 1) | **Hours** Galleria: Tue–Sun 9:30am–7:30pm, Thu till 10:30pm;
Caveau: every third Thursday of the month, 5pm–9pm (guided tours must be booked:
Associazione Civita, Tel +39 0243353525) | **Tip** From the same entrance and for free
you can visit the 18th-century Palazzo Anguissola, rich in decorations. Here are
exhibited the works of many 19th-century landscape artists who depicted Milan and
Lombardy. As you exit there is a bar/restaurant that is a good place to relax.

35 __ Giardini della Guastalla

Milan's oldest pocket of green

It can certainly be said that Milan's youth has good taste, if when they play hooky (*bigiare*, as they say in Milan) they head to the Giardini della Guastella, a picturesque pocket of green and also the first city park, acquired by the city council in 1938. It hasn't changed much since then. So take a stroll under the perfumed branches of linden and beech trees, or along the pathways, hedges, fountains, and flowerbeds that surround the beautiful giant Baroque fishpond, set within a low marble-columned balustrade. Until a few years ago, you could see the fish skimming around the water lilies. Dogs are welcome, and there's a lovely children's playground.

The park is a typical example of an Italian Renaissance garden, designed in the style of the Lombard "villas of delight," though it actually was originally an all-girls boarding school, founded by the countess Guastella to provide an education to the daughters of those impoverished noble families who were unable to pay for it.

The botanical area is particularly interesting, as well as the perfect setting for a romantic stroll, with over forty varieties of trees, including plane trees, magnolias, and tulip trees. There are various statues scattered here and there, and even a neoclassical temple. Needless to say, graffiti artists have spray-painted their signatures all over the building; a real shame. There is also a 17th-century niche that houses a group sculpture in terra-cotta depicting Mary Magdalene comforted by angels.

The historic garden is just behind the old hospital of the Ca' Granda, today the University of Milan, and on sunny days it is not uncommon to see young women lying on benches sunbathing, groups of students having sandwiches, or work colleagues taking a break for some fresh air.

This is truly a delightful place for a rest – as long as you can find a free bench.

Address Via Francesco Sforza, 20121 Milan | **Getting there** Largo Augusto (tram 12, 23, 37); Sforza Ospedale (bus 94) | **Hours** Nov–Feb 7am–7pm, Mar 7am–8pm, Apr 7am–9pm, May–Sep 7am–10pm, Oct 7am–9pm | **Tip** On the other side of the street are the ruins of the Ponte dell'Ospedale ("hospital bridge") that crossed the old Naviglio (now paved over), linking the hospital – today the University of Milan – to the cemetery in Rotonda della Besana.

36_ Giardini di Villa Reale

Where you must be accompanied by a child

The sign at the entrance is clear: to enter you have to be younger than 12 years old, or else be accompanied by a child. The delightful gardens of Via Palestro, next to the Gallery of Modern Art, are an unexpected oasis of tranquility, designed at the end of the 18th century by the Viennese architect Leopoldo Pollak for the wife of Count Lodovico Barbiano di Belgiojoso. Take a stroll among the park's large trees, along the stone-lined pathways that flank the lake, and over the wooden bridges and hillocks – all deliberately designed to create a landscape that is both varied and natural-looking, typical of an English garden.

There's a bit of everything here: woodlands and a variety of plants and trees, such as cedar, cherry, plane, and hackberry; statues; fake ruins; and even a classical temple for the delight of the noblewomen who came here in search of some shade from the sun to protect their porcelain-white skin.

Only as one nears the villa does the lawn become wide and sunny, to allow the natural light to penetrate the building through the large windows and illuminate the interior. The effect is a real eye-catcher, with the whole façade exalting the neoclassical elegance of the villa – so rationally sumptuous that Napoleon Bonaparte chose it as his Milanese residence.

But this is of little interest to the children, who prefer the water channels that flow into the lake, and its mallards and other ducks.

Among the rocking horses and swings of the small playground, you can catch a glimpse of the white life-size statues created by Fausto Melotti, half hidden by the trees. The sculpture, entitled *I Sette Savi* (The Seven Wise Men), denotes an area shared with the Contemporary Art Pavilion. It is the only place where adults – or the odd person or two who didn't catch the sign at the entrance – may enter unaccompanied by a child.

Address Via Palestro 14, 20121 Milan | Getting there Palestro (M1 red line); Cavour (bus 61, 94) | Hours Daily, Nov–Apr 9am–4pm, May–Oct 9am–7pm | Tip In the public gardens in front is the Biolab, an interactive "garden of sciences" for children, located in the former greenhouse of Palazzo Dugnano (the entrance is at Via Daniele Manin 2/a, open daily 9am–1pm, 1:30–5pm).

37__Giorgio Strehler
The revolution of the Piccolo Teatro

May 14, 1947: Paolo Grassi, Giorgio Strehler, and Nina Vinchi unveil the country's first municipal theater in Milan, marking the beginning of a full-blown cultural revolution.

Its manifesto declared: "We do not believe that theater is simply a respectable expression of worldly habits or an abstract homage to culture." And so a theater finally came to the city, as a place where the community could come together and relive the tragedy of *King Lear* in the Renaissance splendor of the Palazzo del Broletto.

Today you can reach Piccolo Teatro from Via Dante. Passing in front of it, it is almost impossible to resist the urge to go inside, have a coffee, and check out the program, which always showcases the latest trends in experimental theater. For its debut, the Piccolo put on Gorky's *The Lower Depths*, and since then it has continued along those intelligent and unpredictable lines, jumping from Goldoni to García Lorca, from Shakespeare's tragedies to Chekhov's realism, from Brecht's epic dramas to Genet's love of the absurd. It is a "theatre for everyone," as one of its most famous slogans recited, which has not lost its democratic, civic, and social vocation.

But one thing has to be said: the Piccolo Teatro is Strehler, and Strehler is the Piccolo Teatro. The two have never been apart, except for a short period at the end of the 1960s, when the director left to found the Cooperativa Teatro Azione. Up until 1998 he directed 200 of the 300 performances staged, before being succeeded by Sergio Escobar and then Luca Ronconi.

His name is still on the posters, and there are now three Piccoli theaters: the Grassi (the original 488-seat theater), the Strehler (the newest one, with almost 1000 seats), and the Studio (368 seats), which also houses the drama school. To further discuss theater over a cup of coffee, head over to the bar in the cloister of Palazzo Broletto.

Address Via Rovello 2, 20121 Milan, Tel +39 848800304, www.piccoloteatro.org | Getting there Cairoli and Cordusio (M 1 red line); Cairoli (tram 1); Dante (tram 16, 27) | Hours Ticket office Mon–Sat 9:45am–6:45pm, Sun 1–6:30pm | Tip At Corso Garibaldi 17 you can see the old façade of the Teatro Fossati, now the Piccolo Teatro Studio (accessible from Via Rivoli), which was the first theater to have electricity.

38__Giovanni Sacchi Archive

Designer and artisan

It's hard to imagine a better location for an archive displaying the work of an artisan who has created some of the past century's most iconic household accessories. From the revolutionary "Grillo" telephone, designed by Marco Zanuso for Siemens, to the famous "Mirella" sewing machine designed by Marcello Nizzoli, which was awarded the prestigious *Compasso d'oro* prize in 1957 – it was Giovanni Sacchi's hands that gave life to a number of the inventions that, from the 1960s onward, went on to enrich the lives of many households, and not just in Italy. The archive is a reminder of a time long gone, when designer and artisan together forged a creative synergy that accompanied every stage of the object's development and production.

This extraordinary collection is hosted in the MIL – Museo dell'Industria e del Lavoro (Museum of Industry and Labor). Some of Sacchi's works are on display at the entrance, but the real gem of the collection is found on the first floor, where the artisan's laboratory – containing 400 wooden models and 8,000 drawings – has been recreated down to the smallest detail. At first sight it looks like the old workshop of a second-hand dealer, with an array of objects scattered like abandoned toys around the dusty, badly lit shelves. But old junk this is not: a closer look reveals each of these pieces as an exceptional work of art, worthy of the MoMA. This is confirmed by the large panel located at the entrance, scribbled on which are the autographs of the carpentry shop's most famous clients: Achille Castiglioni, Aldo Rossi, Gae Aulenti, and many others – in other words, everyone who was anyone in the world of design from the 1940s up until 1997, when the Sacchi workshop closed.

The surrounding garden is dominated by the massive bridge crane of the Ansaldo steel factory, which once operated the place – a striking contrast to the petite Alessi Moka pots on display inside.

Address MIL-Archivio Sacchi, Via Granelli 1, 20099 Sesto San Giovanni (MI), Tel +39 0236682271, www.archiviosacchi.it | Getting there Bignami (M 5 lilac line); Sesto Rondò (M 1 red line) | Hours Tue–Fri 10am–6pm | Tip In the garden, check out the old Brera locomotive of 1906 and the Muro delle voci (Wall of voices), a piece of musical art that reproduces the sound of thousands of laborers at work in the old factory. Ask the custodians to activate it.

39__Hangar Bicocca

From steel factory to contemporary art laboratory

The creativity of an artist juxtaposed with the impersonal machinery of a factory: this is the theme in *Sequenza* (Sequence), Fausto Melotti's iron sculpture positioned at the entrance to the Breda steel factory. For almost a century – beginning in 1886 – thousands of steelworkers gathered here every morning to begin their workday. A lot has changed since then: today the redbrick gabled buildings host exhibitions, art labs, and avant-garde video performances. The grandchildren of the workers who once toiled for Ansaldo, Falk, and Magneti Marelli now come to the bistro, notable for its colorful designer tables, for happy hour.

Even with the passage of time and change of purpose, a strange atmosphere still lingers in this former factory district, as if the walls and gray avenues still exude labor and fatigue. A small door opens into a 100,000-square-foot hangar, which houses the monumental work by Anselm Kiefer, *I Sette Palazzi Celesti* (The Seven Celestial Palaces). Inside the giant nave, in semidarkness, seven towers rise up to 60 feet in height like dilapidated skyscrapers made of piled-up shacks, cement, and war debris.

The impressive installation was inspired by an ancient Hebrew text about a man's spiritual journey in search of God. Clearly, the artist believes that humanity still has a long way to go, and this informs his view of the 20th century – one of war, avant-garde movements, urban growth, and industrial revolutions.

But little is left today of the old city of steel, the "Italian Stalingrad" – famous for the processions of red flags that would gather in front of the Duomo, the blast furnaces, the control rooms, the nuts and bolts; gone is the echo of the 1943 strikes that sent so many workers to the Nazi concentration camps.

For a trip down memory lane, wait for a sunny day and take a (guided) bicycle ride through the industrial area.

Address Via Chiese 2, 20122, Tel +39 0266111573 Milan, www.hangarbicocca.org |
Getting there Ponale (M 5 lilac line); Sarca / Chiese (bus 728) | Hours Wed 12 – 3:30pm,
Thu – Sun 11 – midnight; bicycle tours are organized by HB Tour every Sunday, advance
booking is required (check the website) | Tip At Viale dell'Innovazione 20 is the
modern Teatro degli Arcimboldi, a veritable "theater workshop" and music store
(www.teatroarcimboldi.it), conceived by Vittorio Gregotti.

40__HUB

The creativity of Barbara Zucchi

Two shop fronts on the Naviglio are full of colored textile scraps, where an old granite column separates two brick arches supporting the vaulted ceiling of the historic palazzo. There are tables, sewing machines, cloth racks, clothes hangers, scissors, spools of thread, and paper and grosgrain patterns, as well as finished articles for sale, such as cushions, aprons, towels, and tote bags – gorgeous, unique, creative, and all handmade.

A boutique that is a cross between a tailor's shop and an art gallery, a clothing store and a workshop – this is how Barbara Zucchi, heir to one of the most important textile groups in the industry, has decided to preserve the family tradition, while giving it a modern twist.

The name, Hub Textile, is not a coincidence: the idea is to salvage the creative craft of sewing, which once belonged to the Italian grandmothers, and now, at least in Milan, has mostly been taken over by small entrepreneurs from Eastern Europe, who for a few coins will shorten trousers or tighten skirts and the like.

Hub is a whole different story: here you can have a chat with the "handywomen," Cecilia and Francesca, and even use the shop's equipment to sew, cut, and dye the material yourself, and literally create your own design. The seamstresses will gladly offer their advice, and if you're a novice, you can sign up for one of the workshops that take place around the large table in the rear of the store.

In the back room, the wooden and metal blocks of the Zucchi collection, dating from the end of the 19th century, are available for embellishing the material. From decorative printing to workshops of all sorts, the possibilities are practically endless, even for children.

You can sew a fancy present, write a catchy phrase on a T-shirt, decorate a blanket, and even throw an unusual party for your friends, in a whirlwind of cloth, needles, and felt-tip pens.

Address Ripa di Porta Ticinese 69, 20143 Milan, Tel +39 0245548183, www.l-hub.it |
Getting there Porta Genova (M 2 green line); Porta Genova (tram 2) | **Tip** At Via
Vigevano 32, across from the Porta Genova station, you can find the Self Service dello
Scampolo (self-service remnants shop), a store frequented by students of the fashion
school looking for cheap materials.

41 Idroscalo
The Milanese sea

How do the Milanese cool off in the sweltering heat of summer, since the closest beach is miles away? They head down to the Idroscalo, of course! The first visit is always a bit of a shock, but you soon get used to the lines of beach umbrellas, sun beds, picnic tables, and towels stretched out on the grass bank of this large artificial lake.

On Saturdays and Sundays, Milan's favorite sports park gets crowded – and rightly so. This vast, green expanse is the perfect place to dive into nature and take a breath of clean air; there's simply nothing else like it in town, unless you want to flee the city Friday night to spend the weekend on the beach (a real one). But you will pay for it dearly come Sunday, when thousands of cars line up on the highway to head home.

Some come here for an outdoor snack, others to sunbathe or to jog. There are running tracks and tennis courts, swimming pools with dizzying slides, climbing walls, swings for kids, roller-skating circuits, a rugby field, and enough lawn to satisfy your greenest fantasies.

It is just outside the city, close to Linate Airport. This is where the hydroplanes would once fly in and out, and this was the lake's original function when it was built, in 1962, when Northern Italy was at the forefront of the hydroplane revolution. Today only the Como flying club, the oldest in Europe, is still operational. The seaplane base here suffered a less glorious fate: it was closed soon after its opening and converted into a recreational area.

Fed by the waters of the Martesana Naviglio and a local spring, Idroscalo began being used for canoe racing in 1934. It finally entered triumphantly into the city's collective imagination when, in 1960, Luchino Visconti filmed the most famous scene from *Rocco and His Brothers* here, starring Alain Delon. That sad, ferocious scene is a far cry from the joyous park that it is today.

Address Via Circonvallazione Idroscalo (Strada Provinciale 14 Linate Airport), various entrances, 20090 Segrate (MI), Tel +39 0270208197, www.idroscalo.info | **Getting there** Bus 73 from San Babila to Linate Airport; Villetta-Tribune-Punta dell'Est-Bosco Nord (bus 183); Sat and Sun Linate (bus 930); on Sunday bus 73 continues to the Idroscalo | **Hours** Summer: 7am–9pm. Winter: 7am–5pm | **Tip** In the eastern section (entrance 3 – Punta dell'Est) there is a park with a permanent collection of sculptures and open-air works by artists such as Giacomo Manzù, Luciano Minguzzi, and Paolo Delle Monache, in collaboration with the Accademia di Brera and the Permanente.

42_ The Interactive Museum of Cinema

Look who's talking!

It is like taking a trip back in time when you exit the hyper-modern lilac metro line and enter the rationalist building that once housed a tobacco factory – and still sports the original sign on its façade.

As soon as you step inside, you are instantly transported to the black-and-white world of the Lumière brothers. This is just the beginning of a wondrous journey among puppets, old instruments, and monitors that reproduce memorable films and historic documentaries.

There is an archive of thousands of reels, 30 hours of footage that can be viewed on interactive screens, and more that 100 vintage items ranging from movie cameras to magic lanterns. Have fun dubbing your voice for that of Robert De Niro's, and then e-mail yourself the recording; enjoy a trip down memory lane to the Futurist Milan of the 1920s, in the company of Marinetti, Balla, and Depero; or get to know Italo Pacchioni, who brought cinematography to Milan when he filmed the funeral of Giuseppe Verdi in 1901.

Then you have the "talking wardrobes" film archives: just insert an index card and – *presto* – the requested film appears. The wealth of material available is astonishing: from the work of the Italian film stars of the 1920s, to the commercials of the 1970s.

An illuminated map allows you to zoom in on the geographical location, city, neighborhood, or piazza where some of the most famous scenes of Italian cinema were shot, and experience the emotion of being on the set with Fellini or Visconti (elsewhere in the museum you can view signed sketches and designs by these and other famous directors).

Finally, you can listen to someone's opinion or give your own: just stand on the footprints in front of the *Senti chi parla* sign and have a conversation with whatever film star appears in the hologram.

Address Viale Fulvio Testi 121, 20162 Milan, Tel +39 0287242114,
www.cinetecamilano.it | Getting there Bicocca (M 5 lilac line; tram 7, 31) |
Hours Mon–Fri 3–6pm, Sun 3–7pm, every Sunday guided tours at 4:30pm | Tip
At Porta Venezia, at Viale Vittorio Veneto 2, there is the Oberdan cinema, run
by the Cineteca (Milan's film archive), which puts on retrospectives of quality films
(oberdan.cinetecamilano.it).

43_Isola di Frida

The hipster district that is almost extinct

North of the iron railroad tracks of the Porta Garibaldi Station is a district called Isola (meaning "island") – appropriately so, since it is isolated, suspended in time, separated from the rest of the city, and rather hipster-ish.

Lately, with the rise of the nearby skyscrapers of Porta Nuova – which house the new seat of the regional government and the head office of Unicredit Bank – the city council has began to clean up the neighborhood a bit. Most would see this as a good thing, but Stefania begs to differ.

She misses the squatters who have been evicted from their historic locations, and sensing what the future might hold, fears that Isola's pavements will be transformed into yet another Corso Como, with its happy hours for models and soccer stars.

To emphasize the point – and to make sure that visitors know what to expect – a mural of scribbles greets you at the entrance to Frida, an eclectic and offbeat hybrid between a shop and a café. Stefania runs a store here, Particelle Complementari, where you'll find an incredible range of objects, selected and laid out with exceptional taste: modern antiques, T-shirts, sustainable clothing, and even an original 1950s fridge used as a wardrobe. In the charming courtyard are café tables where people come for coffee, a hot plate of food, or to meet up with friends. Just in front of the warehouse (originally a chair factory) is the aperitif counter, made from 1960s-style majolica tiles.

As you can imagine, the notion of eco-sustainability is central to Frida's philosophy, as exemplified by the wood floor and tables designed by the Controprogetto studio, which is known for using recycled materials. Also important to the concept of Frida is the establishment's relationship with the local community. Among the many noteworthy initiatives is the Clown Festival, held every year during Carnival week, and not to be missed.

Address Via Antonio Pollaiuolo 3, 20159 Milan, Tel +39 02680260, www.fridaisola.it | **Getting there** Garibaldi (M2 green line); Isola (M5, lilac line); Lambertenghi (tram 33); Lagosta (tram 7); Traù/Lagosta (bus 60) | **Hours** Mon–Fri 10am–3pm/ 6pm–2am, Sat 4pm–2am, Sun 12pm–1am | **Tip** At Via Gaetano de Castillia 26, there is the Stecca degli Artigiani, where several associations have their offices, among them a bicycle workshop that lets you use its equipment and expertise free of charge to mend your own bike (www.piubici.org).

44__Jacaranda
The shop window of a rock 'n' roll luthier

It's not every day that you see a shop window displaying actual "luthiers" – that is, makers of stringed instruments such as guitars and basses – hard at work just behind the counter. But this is not your everyday shop. And Daniele and Davide, who combine their expertise and sensibility with a great love of rock 'n' roll, are not your everyday lute makers.

It all started when Daniele Fierro met the Milanese luthier Carlo Raspagni, an old friend of some of Italy's greatest 20th-century musicians, such as Luigi Tenco, Enzo Jannacci, Fabrizio De André, and Adriano Celentano, to name but a few. In 1999, Daniele opened Jacaranda with his friend Luca, with the aim of combining their artisanal skills with their passion for plucked instruments. "Today we mainly make bass and electric guitars, but we repair all sorts of string instruments: lutes, mandolins, ukuleles," says Daniele, pointing to the instrument being fixed by Davide Fossati (Fossati graduated from the Civica Scuola di Liuteria di Milano, class of 1985).

Jacaranda has become a point of reference for enthusiasts, musicians, and collectors, but it is also a place where people come by just to have a peek, thanks also to the shop's location, situated in the lively area of the Navigli. Among the many friends (and clients) who are regulars here: the bass player and producer Saturnino Celani; the guitarist Luigi Schiavone; the violinist (and instrument collector) Mario Pagani; and last but not least, the king of the Milanese jazz scene, Gigi Cifarelli.

You'll find them chatting away about the latest musical trends with Daniele and Davide, who remain faithful to their original plan: to design personalized instruments even for the most demanding musicians.

Why "Jacaranda" you may ask? Because it is the best wood for making classical guitars: a Brazilian rosewood, now a protected species.

Address Via Corsico 8, 20144 Milan, Tel +39 028394686, www.jacaranda.it |
Getting there Porta Genova (M2 green line; tram 2) | **Hours** Tue–Fri 3:30–7pm,
Sat 9:30am–3pm | **Tip** For lovers of food (and drink), there is the Michelin-starred
Osteria Al Pont de Fer, at Corso di Porta Ticinese 55, run by a highly knowledgeable
"wine lady" (Mon–Sun lunch and dinner, Tel +39 0289406277).

45 _ Jamaica

A bohemian hangout for the artists of Brera

If you want to breathe in the true air of Brera – the favorite neighborhood of Milan's young and often penniless artists and creative types – visit the only bar that has remained loyal to its bohemian past, Jamaica, taken over by Carlo Mainini in 1911. It's easy to miss these days, under siege from a deluge of tourist bars and bistros that have invaded the pavements of Via Brera with their tables and umbrellas.

Close to the Brera Academy of Fine Arts, this is the legendary watering hole where the city's most eccentric crowd would come to while away the evening hours before hopping over to the nearby brothel Via dei Fiori Chiari 17. During the day, though, the Jamaica would morph into a perfectly respectable bar, where academy professors and newspaper directors – even Mussolini, when he was the editor of *Il Popolo d'Italia* – would come for their cappuccino.

In 1948, management of the bar was taken over by Carlo's son, Elio, who transformed it into a meeting place for artists and literati, organizing displays and exhibitions (still a tradition today) that attracted the likes of the poets Quasimodo and Ungaretti, the artists Ennio Morlotti and Lucio Fontana, the writers Nanni Balestrini and Antonio Recalcati, the photographer Ugo Mulas, and of course Dario Fo.

The family tradition is continued by Micaela, who has remained faithful to the spirit of the place. The old wooden counter and worn flooring are still there, and the prices haven't spiked simply because Brera has today become hip. Thanks to Micaela, Jamaica remains a symbol of resistance, impervious to modernity.

This is a slice of Milan that is in danger of becoming extinct, where you can still buy a *cotoletta alla milanese* at two in the morning and talk culture. The only novelty is the first-floor restaurant, with its black-and-white photos from the 1950s, when people came here to play cards and gamble.

Address Via Brera 32, 20121 Milan, Tel +39 02876723, www.jamaicabar.it | Getting there Montenapoleone (M3 red line); Lanza (M2 green line); San Marco (bus 61) | Hours Mon–Sun 8am–2am | Tip At Via dei Fiori Scuri 13, you can still see the writing in terra-cotta belonging to the old pharmacy that Carlo Erba took over in 1937, giving birth to Italy's first pharmaceutical company, which also conducted important research on cannabis.

46 La Scala Shop

A treasure trove for opera lovers

At first glance, it appears to be a museum gift shop like all others, filled with merchandise, trinket boxes, and delightful odds and ends that are as useless as they are aesthetically alluring; a happy combination of creative design and centuries-old traditions (the well-known logo of the Teatro La Scala appears on pretty much everything).

If you're a fan of opera, you're bound to find something that takes your fancy: a key ring with the iconic poster of the 1952 production of Puccini's *La Bohème*; a pen holder signed "La Scala 1778"; a reproduction of Giuseppe Verdi's paperweight; or a puzzle that depicts the façade of the theater, painted by Angelo Inganni in 1852. And then there are writing materials of all kinds, cups, T-shirts, bags, and clutches designed with scenes and verses from *Aida* or *La Traviata*. More "modern" items include a red-lined tablet case and a mouse pad with the poster of the 1966 production of *Nabucco*.

There's always something to be found in this half chic, half kitsch treasure trove, but to ferret out the real goodies you need to go downstairs. This is where things start to get serious: the shelves are filled with books about music, dance, and opera, but there are also illustrated volumes that allow children to cut out and assemble famous stage clothes and learn about the different characters along the way. There are also black-and-white photographs for sale that chronicle La Scala's glorious past: its collaboration with Arturo Toscanini, and the 1950s debut of Maria Callas, "la divina," whose miraculous voice left the audience agape; and CDs galore of the most famous operas, including the special (and precious) editions produced by La Scala.

You will also discover treasures of another era, like the vinyl reprint of the legendary recording of Antonín Dvořák's *Cello Concerto n.2 in B minor*, performed by Rostropovich – an LP for the true connoisseur.

Address Piazza della Scala (next door to the theater), 20121 Milan, Tel +39 0245483257, www.lascalashop.it | **Getting there** Duomo (M1 red line and M1 yellow line); Manzoni (tram 1) | **Hours** Mon–Sun 10:30am–7:30pm | **Tip** The Caffè Biffi, in the Galleria Vittorio Emanuele, apart from being one of the oldest in Milan (1867), is where Callas, Toscanini, and Nureyev, as well as the regular theatergoers, would stop for a drink after the concerts at La Scala.

47__The Legend of the Female Boar

A tale that the Milanese would happily forget

Just as the wolf is symbolic of Rome, so the *scrofa semilanuta* ("half-woolen boar") is the emblem of Milan, dating back – according to a local legend – to the very founding of the city. Not a noble beast, to say the least, given that it belongs to the swine family, which may explain why there are so few depictions of it.

In Milan, the *scrofa semilanuta* is only found in two places: in the marble bas-relief of a capital supporting one of the arches of the Palazzo della Ragione in the magnificent Piazza dei Mercanti, and in the coat of arms engraved in the courtyard of Palazzo Marino.

The legend, as recounted by Livy, is rather endearing. It seems that in the 6th century BC the Celtic king, Ambicatus, sent his two nephews on a mission to colonize new territories. Up to this point, the tale is faithful to history: it's true that at that time some Insubric tribes from Gaul crossed over the Alps and reached Italy. From here, however, the story veers from fact to fiction.

One of the brothers, Bellovesus, had a vision: a female boar with the front part of its body covered in long fur (hence *semilanuta* – "half woolen") grazing in a fertile glade near two streams. The Celts considered the female boar to be a sacred animal, so much so that it was engraved on Bellovesus's shield. The soldier interpreted the vision as an auspicious sign from the gods and an invitation to build a new city. He named it *Medhe-lan*, which in Gallic means "middle land" or "middle flatland," which later evolved into the Latin *Mediolanum*, meaning "semi-woolen."

But there is a mystery in all this: the bas-relief on the capital is older than the palazzo itself, which was built in the 13th century AD; maybe it was found during excavations for the new building and used as decoration. Today, few people passing by take notice of it.

Address Piazza dei Mercanti, 20122 Milan | **Getting there** Duomo (M 1 red line e M 3 yellow line); Cordusio (tram 12, 14, 16) | **Tip** Under the arches you can test an acoustic effect which was used by the merchants to talk to each other without being overheard. All you have to do is find two oblique columns with a hole in them: if you talk into one hole you can be heard from the other.

48_Lucio Fontana's Neon Lights

The glow that illuminates the Duomo

The two rationalist-style buildings of the Palazzo dell'Arengario, situated in front of the Duomo, stand in stark contrast to the aesthetic excesses of the cathedral. The basilica's eccentricity must have been a real eyesore for the Fascist architects of the 1930s, who tried to transform the most Baroque of Milan's piazzas into a stage for Il Duce's speeches. The 1937 buildings were conceived by the architects Portaluppi, Muzio, Magistretti, and Griffini, while the ornamentation on the façade of the palazzo is by Arturo Martini.

If you look closely, you will notice that the two square towers are directly in line with the arch of the Galleria Vittorio Emanuele, on the opposite side of the piazza. The outer walls are covered in the same precious marble from Candoglia that was used five centuries earlier in the construction of the Duomo. At the time, its transportation to Milan required the construction of a system of canals, the Navigli, reaching well into the city center. Today this austere, rationalist style, less somber than that of other buildings of the time, actually appears remarkably modern.

The structure is softened by a series of windows on two floors that illuminate its interior, now a museum dedicated to the 20th century. Light is the dominant element of the piazza: it filters through from the Art Nouveau glass windows of the Galleria Vittorio Emanuele into the white marble of the basilica, which reflects the sun by day and the moon by night.

Another source of light was added in 2011. Lucio Fontana's fluorescents, originally designed by the artist in 1951 for the staircase of the Palazzo della Triennale, are 430 feet of neon lighting that twist like arabesques. They hang from the ceiling, and in the evening their light shines through the windows and out onto the piazza.

Address Piazza Duomo, 20122 Milan, www.museodelnovecento.org | Getting there
Duomo (M1 red line and M3 yellow line) | Hours Mon 2:30–7:30pm; Tue, Wed,
Fri, and Sun 9:30am–7:30pm; Thu and Sat 9:30am–10:30pm (there is no admittance
one hour before closing). | Tip At Corso Monforte 19 is the Artemide showroom,
famous for its designer lamps, and at Via San Damiano 3 is the Guzzini showroom,
specializing in kitchen utensils.

49__ The Maggiolina
The mushroom houses

Among the city's northern suburban avenues, built at the beginning of the 20th century to connect Milan to Monza, there is a residential area that is striking for its beauty as well as for the extravagance of its houses: the Maggiolina and the adjacent Villaggio dei Giornalisti (Journalists' Village), so named because it was designed by a cooperative of editors, writers, and journalists. It all started with a polemical op-ed by the editor of *Il Secolo* in 1911, in which he accused the government of focusing only on public housing and the urban needs of the working classes, while ignoring the middle-class districts.

Today the Maggiolina is a picturesque garden city with quiet tree-lined streets and beautiful Art Nouveau-style villas, whose walls are decorated with arabesques, towers, and balconies.

It's almost like traveling to a different time and place, as removed as possible – both psychologically and acoustically – from the traffic and noisy shopping centers of the nearby Viale Zara.

Villa Mirabello is a magnificent example of a suburban fifteenth-century farmstead, now converted into private offices; fortunately, you can still glimpse it from the outside by walking around the fence.

However, the most original urban experiment is on Via Lepanto, behind the railway tracks, where the engineer Mario Cavallè, built a series of mushroom- and igloo-shaped houses just after the war.

The project was less bizarre than you might think. The idea was to build temporary housing units as a quick response to the growing needs of families forced out of their homes by the bombing raids during the war. But the cupola houses, each one with its own garden, were so pretty that they remained. There was talk of demolishing them in the 1960s but a petition circulated by Luigi Figini, an architect who lived in the neighborhood, prevented this from happening.

Address Via Lepanto and Via Villa Mirabello, 20125 Milan | **Getting there** Marche and Istria (M5 lilac line); Farina (bus 42); Zara/Laurana (tram 5, 7) | **Tip** A few feet away from the mushroom houses, at Via Perrone di San Martino 8, is the Palafitta ("stilt house"), the villa designed by the architect Luigi Figini in the rationalist style of the 1930s, so called because it is built on pillars.

50 Manzoni's Study

Where the writer penned his masterpiece

Milan is so full of Alessandro Francesco Tommaso Antonio Manzoni that you won't know where to begin. A good starting point, though, is the last house where the Italian poet and novelist lived, on Via Morone. He bought the place in 1813.

If you read Manzoni's biography you will realize how nomadic his life was: he lived in Lecco, Venice, and Paris. But however hard his father, a Lecce nobleman, tried to keep him away from such a "dissolute and democratic" city, Manzoni always found his way back to his birthplace: Milan. A true patriot, he fought vehemently against the city's foreign invasions, testified to by the commemorative plaque in Piazza San Fedele, where he roused the crowd during the 1848 revolt. His commitment soon made him a well-loved figure in the city, and earned him a place of honor among the pantheon of celebrities in the Cimitero Monumentale.

He is considered the father of the historical novel, and the small walnut desk where he wrote his masterpiece, *I Promessi Sposi* (*The Betrothed*) – set in Milan during the 17th century, when the city was under Spanish rule and besieged by famine and plague – can still be seen in his old study overlooking Piazza Belgioioso.

One can imagine his wife bringing him tea there, as Manzoni dipped his pen into his inkwell to write the story of Renzo, the love-struck peasant boy who enters the city in the middle of a revolt. Upon reaching the Duomo, Renzo is immediately confronted with the "arrogance of power," as he witnesses the tragic episode of the "column of infamy." This moment in history is also recalled on a headstone at the Sforza Castle, as well as on the façade of the house of the barber who was unjustly accused of spreading the plague and executed in Corso di Porta Ticinese. In the Lazzaretto – the district near Porta Venezia – Renzo is finally reunited with his beloved Lucia. This epic story is Manzoni's homage to his city.

Address Via Gerolamo Morone 1, 20121 Milan, Tel +39 0286460403,
www.casadelmanzoni.it | **Getting there** Duomo and San Babila (M 1 red line); Duomo
and Montenapoleone (M 3 yellow line) | **Hours** Tue – Fri (closed on bank holidays)
9am – 4pm | **Tip** In Piazza Belgioioso – or more precisely inside the sumptuous Palazzo
Belgioioso – is the Boeucc, one of the most elegant (in the classic sense of the word)
restaurants in town, sporting a columned room with a vaulted ceiling, parquet floor,
long tablecloths, crystal glassware, and silver cutlery (www.boeucc.it).

51 Marinetti's House

The "home" of Futurism

Unfortunately it's hardly noticeable, but at the corner of Corso Venezia and Via Senato, you can find a plaque honoring the first house of Filippo Tommaso Marinetti (1876–1944) – one of the main figures of the 20th-century artistic avant-garde and the founder of Futurism. The city really should show greater respect for the man, despite his frenzied and boisterous exploits (such as his over-the-top and rather aggressive street and theater performances, during which he incited people to revolt "against ecstasy and sleep").

Marinetti was a poet, playwright, artist, and above all, activist. He was at the forefront of a revolutionary movement like nothing that had ever come before, and which counted among its members Umberto Boccioni, Giacomo Balla, Carlo Carrà, and numerous other intellectuals and artists.

The "eastern salon of the Egyptian bard" (Marinetti was born in Alexandria, Egypt) on Corso Venezia was where the magazine *Poesia* (*Poetry*) was published. Founded in 1905, it exalted the freedom and dynamism of a language liberated from the shackles of syntax. The location became a regular hangout for celebrities and musicians, such as Igor Stravinsky and the film and opera director, Don Luchino Visconti, conte di Modrone.

It is a real shame to think that the publication of the novel *Mafarka il Futurista*, in 1910, created such an uproar among Milan's well-to-do that Marinetti was arrested for indecency and imprisoned for several days in the San Vittore jail. That same year the *Manifesto dei Pittori Futuristi* (Manifesto of the Futurist Painters) was also launched. It set out the principles of the movement; an ideology that was at once dynamic and destructive (it wholeheartedly supported the case for war: "We want to demolish all the museums, libraries and academies of all sorts." Which means if it had been up to Marinetti, there wouldn't even be a plaque to remember him.

Address Corso Venezia 21, 20121 Milan | Getting there San Babila (M 1 red line); Senato (bus 61, 94) | Tip Few people notice it, but at Via Senato 10, in front of the Palazzo del Senato, one of the two bronze sculptures is Mere Ubu, the work of the celebrated Spanish surrealist Joan Mirò, who in 1973 bequeathed it to the city of Milan.

QUESTA É LA CASA
DOVE NEL 1905

FILIPPO TOMMASO MARINETTI
FONDÒ LA RIVISTA "POESIA"

DA QUI IL MOVIMENTO FUTURISTA
LANCIÒ LA SUA SFIDA
AL CHIARO DI LUNA SPECCHIATO NEL NAVIGLIO

52 Martesana

Cycling along Leonardo da Vinci's Naviglio

The old Navigli – a canal system surrounding Milan – has today been transformed into cycling paths. The locals' favorite is undoubtedly the Martesana, which runs along the canal that connected Milan to the Adda River, in the eastern part of the city. You can actually cycle all the way from the skyscrapers of Porta Nuova to Lecco, on Lake Como. Just follow the river and admire the water basins that Leonardo da Vinci designed, the Visconti castles, and the first hydroelectric plants of the 20th century; cycle under the Paderno d'Adda bridge, a single iron arched viaduct that crosses the two riverbanks of the narrow gorge, an ambitious feat of engineering; and then, at Imbersago, take the ferry, also designed by da Vinci and the only one still in use that relies on the current to move.

To appreciate all this, just head north on Via Melchiorre Gioia until you get to the Cassina de' Pomm, the old tavern covered in wisteria that is now the Caffè Martesana. Here the Naviglio emerges into the open air, flanked by the cycling paths. It is also known as the Naviglio Piccolo ("small Naviglio"), and its 23-mile course has a 60-foot drop in its gradient, which the boats were able to pass thanks to da Vinci's basins.

The boats would enter a side lock, the sluices would close, and water would be pumped in or drained from it until it reached the same level as the external canal. The stretch to Cassina de' Pomm was inaugurated in 1471, while the one that entered the city (now underground) – connecting to the internal navigation circuit at Tombòn de San Marc (Brera) – was finished in 1496.

In the 16th century, the Naviglio was to the Lombard countryside what the railroad was to the American West in the 19th century. Following its creation, farmsteads, hamlets, villas, and inns slowly began to dot the landscape, now much appreciated by today's intrepid cyclists.

Address Via Tirano, 20125 Milan | **Getting there** Gioia/Tirano (bus 43, 81) | **Tip** At Via Cristoforo Gluck 45 is Fermoimmagine, a museum of cinema posters that puts on exhibitions and film festivals. A meeting place for enthusiasts, it also houses the Caffè degli Ignoranti, a library, and a permanent historical archive (www.museofermoimmagine.it, Hours: Tue – Sun 2 – 7pm).

53__Massimo's Ice Cream

Be seduced by Bronte's pistachios

A fairly inconspicuous residential area north of Milan is not where you would expect to find one of the best ice-cream shops in town. But the best things are often hidden in the most unexpected places. The Massimo del Gelato parlor is particularly famous for its pistachio ice cream, which rightfully attracts people from all over the city.

Once inside, you may be momentarily overwhelmed by the 32 flavors available. But it's a good problem to have! Many of the fruit flavors are seasonal, since the products used here are organic and carefully chosen: hazelnuts from Salento in the winter; strawberries in the spring; raspberries, blueberries, and blackberries in the summer; grapes, black and delicious, at harvest time. There are also more exotic flavors, such as Indian mango, so yellow it almost appears fluorescent.

But the pride of this family business is their chocolate flavors, available year-round in eight different varieties: from the Italian *Domori* with a 75-percent cocoa concentration (available with or without liquor) to the Venezuelan *Criollo*, to the "pure gold" (100-percent cocoa, as bitter as it gets); and then there are the chili- and cinnamon-scented varieties, which evoke Lasse Hallström's famous film *Chocolat* (these shameless concoctions of chocolate cream are simply irresistible).

It is equally impossible not to taste the *gianduia* ("nut chocolate"), on which the master ice-cream maker Massimo Travani worked for years to achieve a perfect alchemy between oiliness and smoothness. Almonds from Noto, Sicily; hazelnuts from Piedmont – here the raw materials are everything.

The very delicate *ortigia* cream, made with Sicilian lemons, brings with it the sun and smells of the Mediterranean. The Sicilian *cassata*, rich in candied fruit, is dedicated to the south of Italy and its *joie de vivre*. However, be careful: once you get started it's hard to stop.

I Nostri Cioccolati

Puerto Maya *cioccolato della qualità migliore dei cacaoi*
Domori *fondente amaro per il 75%*
Oro Puro *fondente amaro per il 100%*
Azteca *fondente speziato con peperoncino e cannella*
Elisir *fondente con arancia candita farcita e grand marnier*
Cuvée *fondente con amarena caffè e ricotta*
Jamaica *fondente con rum*
Fiesta Rhum *cioccolato della casa con nocciotine e grand marnier*
Gianduia *cioccolato grand crù e nocciola tonda gentile delle langhe*

Address Via Lodovico Castelvetro 18, 20154 Milan, Tel +39 023494943 | Getting there Sempione / Domodossola or Piero della Francesca / Domodossola (bus 43, 57); Sempione / Arona (tram 1, 19) | Hours Tue – Sat 12-midnight (but closed from Dec 25 to the middle of Feb) | Tip There is a sister ice-cream parlor in Piazza Risorgimento (at Via Pisacane).

54 Milano a Memoria

A 5-D cinematic tour through Milan's history

It doesn't get more central than this: right under the porticoes of Piazza Diaz there is an odd little cinema completely upholstered in red velvet and accessed from a narrow, badly lit corridor. No one is there to welcome you. The wall on the left is lined with cardboard cutouts of Milan's monuments, with labels like *Il Duomo*, *La Scala*, etc.

You may well hesitate before entering, unsettled by the vintage décor of the place, which would not be out of place in a strip club. The atmosphere is even more bewildering if you consider that 15 floors above is the Martini Terrace, the sumptuous haunt of celebrities from the world of TV, culture, and politics. Only at the end of the obscure corridor is the purpose of this curious locale revealed: to preserve the memory of Milan's past.

The foyer, illuminated by a grand crystal chandelier, is filled with books and black-and-white photographs that depict stories of wine and taverns, traditions and dialects. From here you enter into the screening room, where documentaries are shown all day, portraying a Milan that no longer exists, when the city was filled with the eclectic protagonists of the Futurist movement, or when you could get to Brera by boat along the Navigli. Some of the films also include entertaining anecdotes, such as that of the first steam tram.

Quality short films by the likes of Guido Guerrasio, reconstructions of period settings, backstage peaks at La Scala, cabarets, and taverns from the 1950s – there is a vast archive of readily available documentaries that never ceases to amaze, many of which are presented in 3-D and amplified by a hidden mechanism concealed under the wooden seats, which makes the whole room appear to shake as if in an earthquake, and creates "special effects" that simulate rain, wind, and other elements. Anything can happen during this 5-D virtual tour of old Milan.

Address Piazza Armando Diaz 7, 20121 Milan, Tel +39 0249438217,
www.milano-a-memoria-5d.it | Getting there Duomo (M 1 red line, M 3 yellow line) |
Hours Screenings: Tue – Fri and Sun every hour from 10:30am – 4:30pm (in Italian),
from 10am – 4pm (in English); Mon – Sat from 4:30 – 6:30pm (in Italian), from 4 – 6pm
(in English) | Tip Every second Sunday of the month (excluding July and August) a
secondhand book market is held under the porticoes, where you can browse among the
stalls of antique book collectors from all over Italy.

55 Mistero Buffo's Palace

An Art Nouveau stage in an irreverent theater

Only those who live in the vicinity of this beautiful Art Nouveau-style stained-glass-windowed building, immersed in the gardens of largo Marinai d'Italia, are aware of its existence. It was built in 1908 by Migliorini, and was part of the Verziere, the old fruit and vegetable market that was located here until 1965. The fruit stalls, the crowds, the buyers and sellers, the porters in perpetual movement – they all disappeared from one day to the next when the market was moved to its current location.

The building was left empty, until, after many years of neglect, it was occupied in the 1970s by the militant theater company founded by Dario Fo, the 1997 Nobel Prize Laureate in Literature who was, at the time, an emerging and irreverent playwright. Here the comedian rehearsed his most famous play, *Mistero Buffo* (Comical Mystery), which poked fun at the powers that be – at the time, the Christian Democrats, who ruled Italy for 30 years and were hand in glove with the Vatican.

Besides aiming thorny digs at the political leaders of his time, the left-wing scribe also transformed the park and the *palazzina* into an open-air community center rife with initiatives, which he promoted along with his wife, Franca Rama. When Dario Fo climbed onto the stage, as in the tradition of the best court jesters, he used masks and laughter to denounce deception and corruption. During rehearsals, the park would fill with young militants, while the ingenious troubadour would dance like a manic street acrobat, hurling one gibe after another at those in power. Years later, a nationwide judicial investigation into political corruption in the 1990s called the *mani pulite* ("clean hands") would prove that his allegations were not far from the truth.

The square has undergone extensive restoration work, and now boasts an actual stage – a fitting memorial to the master.

Address Parco Vittorio Formentano, largo Marinai d'Italia, 20129 Milan,
Tel +39 023494943 | Getting there Cadore/Anfossi (bus 45, 62, 66); Arconati
(tram 12, 92); Cadore (tram 27, 73) | Hours The park is always open. The palazzina
hosts the chamber orchestra of the Camera Milano Classica and is open only for
concerts and other cultural events. | Tip On the corner of Via Anfossi and Via Cadore
is the Casa del Habano, one of only two tobacconists in Italy that sell Cuban cigars,
which have an exhibition room all for themselves.

56 N'ombra de Vin

The historical wine cellar of the "Milano da bere"

To enter Bacchus's world you have to descend the stairs of the refectory of the former Augustine monastery next to Saint Mark's Basilica, in the Brera Quarter. The 16th-century dining hall has been perfectly preserved; it is divided into two naves, with a cross vault supported in the central part by a row of granite columns. The basement's cool temperature and ancient atmosphere provide the ideal setting for this temple of enology (the science of wine and winemaking).

There are shelves full of bottles and cases of wine everywhere: three thousand labels in total, a third of which are French cru wines; the majority are from Bordeaux and Burgundy. These are the real pride of the Corà family. The cellar is today run by Cristiano, whose father opened it in 1977. He started out selling quality wines to the best restaurants in Milan, and then, after adding a bar for wine pouring and tasting, went on to open what became the favorite cellar of the *Milano da bere* ("Drinkin' Milan"), as the thriving nightlife of the 1980s was called.

To this day, it is considered the "in" place to meet, and the number one of its kind. You can tell when it is time for an aperitif by the crowd that gathers outside the entrance to the wine bar. The wine list, to savor with some hors d'oeuvres before dinner, offers a wide selection of different labels, but there is a clear predilection for Piedmont wines. Topping the list is Barolo, followed by the "super-Tuscans" such as Brunello and Rosso di Montalcino. Downstairs, the original wine shop's old wooden counter is still there, and in a granite basin, various copper cauldrons filled with ice keep the white and sparkling wines ready for serving.

What really sets this place apart from the others is Cristiano Corà's ability to identify the small emerging producers, who often reveal an exceptional – if not always easy on the pocket – winemaking talent.

Address Via San Marco 2, 20121 Milan, Tel +39 026599650, www.nombradevin.it |
Getting there Lanza and Moscova (M2 green line); Pontaccio (bus 61) | **Hours**
Mon–Sat 9am–1:30pm | **Tip** At Via Solferino 27, there is a plaque reminding us
that this is where Giacomo Puccini lived from 1887 to 1900, and where he composed
La Bohème and *Tosca*. You really have to look up to see it.

57_New Old Camera

The vintage courtyard of photography

The dear old camera has found a welcoming home and a collector's showcase in the courtyard belonging to Ryuichi Watanabe, a Japanese orchestra conductor who moved to Italy because of his love for opera. Like many buildings in Milan, this one – located right in the center of town, on Via Dante – has a picturesque hidden courtyard.

As soon as you enter, you are instantly enveloped by the vintage and nostalgic atmosphere of a long-gone black-and-white world. We are talking, of course, of the world of Photography (with a capital *P*), where the art of focusing and snapping are united in the miracle that is the photographic camera.

Zen discipline and poetry are the cardinal principles of Watanabe's philosophy. In fact, Watanabe, who trained as a musicologist, chose Milan because he wanted to perfect the art of the *bel canto*. But the love for all things beautiful spreads like wildfire and Watanabe's passion for singing soon changed to photography, and to one camera in particular: the Leica. In just a few years, Ryuichi transformed this courtyard into a haven (and more) for those who share his interest.

Here you will find an expertise that is truly extraordinary, and a staff of photographers and fixers who handle each lens, each camera body, and each piece of optical equipment as if it were a unique feat of human ingenuity.

People can also come here to sell their old cameras, and find comfort in knowing that they are leaving them in the hands of people who will love them as much as they have. Others come simply to explore an old Milanese courtyard or drool over an ultra-rare Rolleiflex wide-angle with a Zeiss lens or a 1962 Leica M2, among other rarities kept in glass cabinets. Still others come to attend one of the various workshops, view the collection of photographs, or simply chat and exchange ideas with fellow photographers.

Address Via Dante 12, Via Rovello 5, 20121 Milan, Tel +39 0236589216, www.newoldcamera.it | **Getting there** Cairoli and Cordusio (M1 red line); Dante (tram 16, 27); Cairoli (tram 1) | **Hours** Mon 3:30–7pm, Tue–Sat 10am–1pm and 3:30–7pm | **Tip** At Largo Cairoli 2A is the Parallelozero Cafè, run by a photographic agency of well-known photo reporters. They organize exhibitions and meetings of various kinds (check the website: www.parallelozero.com).

58_ Olinda

The garden of creative madness

Even though the last asylum was shut down many years ago, you can still sense the mental distress as you walk along the avenue of linden trees between the different wings of the former psychiatric hospital Paolo Pini. "This is a bit of frontier park," says Rosita, one of the founding partners of the nonprofit company La Fabbrica di Olinda Cooperativa Sociale (Fabric of Olinda Social Cooperative).

She refers to the fact that the place borders one of Milan's seediest neighborhoods, Quarto Oggiaro. But thanks to the work of volunteers like Rosita, the park has become a workshop of ideas, meetings, and creativity that every summer gives birth to a festival rich in events, and is well summed up by their slogan, "Close up, no one is normal."

Everything revolves around the Teatro La Cucina (kitchen theater), located where the institution's kitchen used to be. During the winter months, when there are no shows being put on, the space is offered to theatrical companies looking for a stage to rehearse their productions, and the hostel becomes a guesthouse for actors, clowns, and musicians.

It's a rather bizarre community, but one that fits in with the locals who come to stroll through the avenues, and who no longer notice the Leninist proclamations still hanging on the walls, put up by a former patient affectionately nicknamed the "Bolshevik." The old, gruff rooster who lives on the grounds was so fond of pecking the legs of the new occupants as they worked in the community vegetable garden that he had to be moved to an enclosure.

Tomatoes, peppers, medicinal plants, and other vegetables are grown here – a piece of countryside in the city. Now part of the neighborhood, the park is an example of urban integration, just like Olinda – the invisible city imagined by Italo Calvino that grows in concentric circles so that there are no distinctions between inner and outer neighborhoods.

Address Via Ippocrate 45, 20161 Milan, Tel +39 0266220171, www.olinda.org |
Getting there Affori (M 1 red line) | Hours Mon – Fri 12 – 3pm and when a show is on
from 7:30pm (check the posters or website for the program, www.elfo.org) | Tip In the
city center (Corso Buenos Aires 33), inside the Teatro Elfo Puccini, is Bistrolinda, a
restaurant run by the Olinda co-op, which helps to integrate people with mental issues.
It is always a treat to stop here for lunch or an aperitif before a show.

59__Ombre Rosse

The shop that blends wine and art

The nameplate of this historical wine store is reminiscent of the famous Western film directed by John Ford in 1939 (*Stagecoach* is called *Ombre Rosse* in Italy) but don't for a moment think that you will be entering an Old Western saloon – even if there is a piano on which the owner Raffaella Fossati practices after hours.

The counter is made of wood with a brass top, like in the old days; the only modern touch is the hanging lamp. If you look at the black-and-white pictures hanging on the wall, in which the store is depicted with the same sign that it sports today, you can see that this place dates back at least 100 years.

The wine connoisseur is Federica's husband, Josè Carbonell, who will happily uncork a collectible bottle for his guests, just because he can. The wine-tasting events, accompanied by small but refined menus, are intimate and exclusive affairs, given the limited space of the locale, but this is precisely what makes them such a memorable experience. "Heaven forbid, no happy hours here," the hostess is quick to affirm.

Every evening you can sample four or five wines by the glass. If you're lucky, you might get to taste one of the specialties: a Piedmont Barolo, a red Gaja, a French *cru*. Among the 400 labels in stock, some sell for more than 1,000 euros. But sometimes it can be more fun to gamble on a small producer who might soon be joining the big boys.

Downstairs is Raffaella's creative domain, and her aptly named gallery Fatto ad Arte (Tailor Made). Here she exhibits the work of artisans whose themes are linked to a region, a tradition, a fairy tale, or a specific artist: Caltagirone ceramics, double-sided jugs from Friuli, Murano glass vases, Florentine terra-cotta sculptures, mosaics from Spilimbergo; all made from materials that have been around for centuries, revisited in a modern key. A bit like wine.

Address Via Plinio 29, 20129 Milan, Tel +39 0229524734, www.enotecaombrerosse.com | **Getting there** Lima (M1 red line); Abruzzi/Plinio (bus 92); Eustachi/Plinio (bus 60) | **Hours** Tue–Sat 10am–1pm and 4pm–1am, Mon 6pm–1am | **Tip** In Viale Abruzzi 15 you can relax in the Hammam della Rosa, the only Turkish bath in Milan. It has one area for men, one for women, and one for couples. Skin treatments are also available (Tue–Fri 12–10:30pm, Sat–Sun 10:30am–8.30pm (www.hammamdellarosa.com).

60 Botanico di Brera

A garden of herbs fit for a queen

Finding the Orto Botanico di Brera (the botanical gardens in the Brera Academy) is like being on a treasure hunt. But getting lost in this marvelous 18th-century palazzo has its merits.

The garden is in back of the building under the astronomical observatory, which, from this perspective, looks more like a haunted castle than a science museum. There is a thick tangle of plants that protrude in every direction, as if they are trying to break free, despite the gardeners' efforts to install some order. The most seductive scents come from the flowerbeds dedicated to the medicinal plants, which have grown here for more than 200 years at the service of the Brera "spicery."

If it wasn't for the information board, you would never believe such a narrow space could house 300-plus different species, almost all of them indigenous except for two ginkgo trees, one male and the other female, which are considered among the oldest examples in Europe; the unusual Chinese parasol tree (*Firmiana simplex*); and the giant Caucasian wingnut tree (*Pterocarya fraxinifolia*).

The purpose of the gardens was above all didactic, per the wishes of the empress Maria Theresa of Austria (also queen of Hungary and Bohemia), who in 1774 transformed it into a "Hortus Œcomomicus" to rival the one in Vienna. Her predilection for nature was well known and this delightful oasis is dedicated to her memory.

In the middle of the gardens are the 18th-century elliptic ponds with nymphs designed by the architect Piermarini, who had previously designed the royal palace and the park of Monza for the queen (Milan was under Austrian rule from 1706 to 1797).

The students of the *accademia* know about this haven and often come here to study under the wisteria or the magnolia or to take a romantic stroll while occasionally glancing over to read the Latin names of the various plants on the little placards.

Address Via Privata Fratelli Gabba (at the end of the road), 20121 Milan, Tel +39 0250314680, www.brera.unimi.it | Getting there Montenapoleone (M 3 yellow line); Monte Pietà (bus 61); Manzoni / Montenapoleone (tram 1) | Hours Mon–Fri 9am–12pm and 2–4pm; Sat 10am–4pm | Tip From the courtyard of the academy, at Via Brera 28, it is worth heading up to the first floor and poking your head into the library for a view of its wooden shelves and the entrance to the reading room.

61_Ostello Bello

Let's meet in Carrobbio

Even though Via Torino has become one of the most commercial streets in Milan – from Zara to McDonald's, it's a real brand-fest – you have a better chance of finding traces of the old Milan here than in most other places. For example, some of the original single-window shops – the stationer, the watchmaker – haven't yet thrown in the towel, and you can still see the yellow tram, dating back to 1881, trundle by on its uneven tracks.

This is the Carrobbio District, which had a bad reputation in Manzoni's time but is now right smack in the center of town, just a stone's throw from the Duomo. In fact, the only real danger these days is of being trampled by the tourists and shoppers. Its name derives from the Latin *quadrivium*, which means "a place where four roads meet," because this is where the roads that connected the outskirts to the city center intersected.

Today it is Milan's shopping mecca, overflowing with teenagers and the occasional pickpocket. Which is why it so hard to resist the beckoning of the little silent lane with no shop windows that leads to the Ostello Bello (Pretty Hostel). Inside the building, the seats are made of wooden packing chests that are also used to store towels and sheets, while the walls are covered by a massive collage of newspaper and graffiti – a clever way to cover dirt, explains Pietro, one of the guys who runs the hostel.

There are 10 en suite and air-conditioned rooms, 56 beds, 3 terraces, and an underground living room with guitars, Ping-Pong, and foosball. At happy hour, this wonderfully hippie-minimalist hostel fills up with locals who come here for an aperitif and tourists looking for a place to put their feet up after a long day's walk. Word has gotten around that the happy-hour buffet is abundant and free of charge for those staying at the hostel. That is why the guests call it "free dinner." Hospitality is what Carrobbio is all about.

Address Via Medici 4, 20123 Milan, Tel +39 0236582720, www.ostellobello.com | Getting there Duomo (M 1 red line and M 3 yellow line); Sant'Ambrogio (M 2 green line); Correnti/Carrobbio (tram 2, 14) | Tip Close to Via Torino 32 is the Tempio Civico di San Sebastiano, a civic church with the emblems of the different districts of the city: Romana (red), Ticinese (a red stool), Venezia (a lion), Vercellina (red-and-white stripes), Comasina (red-and-white checks) Nuova (four black-and-white rectangles) and Città di Milano (a red cross on a white background).

62 Osteria del Treno

The award-winning railwaymen's trattoria

This is where the old railway employees' "after work club" was located, next door to the station, and the building still belongs to the Società Nazionale di Mutuo Soccorso (national mutual aid association). It is a rare example of 19th-century (1877) Viennese Art Nouveau-style social architecture. On May 1st, 1898, it became the headquarters of the railway workers' movement. Upstairs, the black-and-white photos and numerous red flags are a reminder of the heated political debates that took place here.

Today, on Sundays, the monumental main room, with its iron columns and finely worked balcony railings, becomes a tango dance floor. On the stage at the end of the room a grand piano stands in splendor, and the tables are laid with elegant white tablecloths and crystal glassware. Angelo Bissolotti, the manager, has organized evening tasting events here since 1989. In 1993, he founded the Milan Slow Food club, with the aim of spreading his passion for the simplicity and excellence of traditional Italian cooking.

You cannot book a table ahead at lunchtime, as Angelo wants to preserve the working-class spirit of the place. The atmosphere is informal and straightforward, just as it would have been in the old days. The menu changes daily and you have to retrieve your food from the chef herself.

Come evening, the vibe changes: the food becomes haute cuisine (and the prices rise accordingly). This is your chance to taste the traditional Lombard *cassoeula* (a casserole made from cabbage and pork), cured meats from the Val d'Orcia (Tuscany), or *alpeggio* cheese tortelli (*alpeggio* refers to the summer grazing of cattle). The goodies all come from different Slow Food *presidia*, or "garrisons": local projects that support Italian products of the highest quality and work to improve the infrastructure of artisan food production. To top off your meal, sample one of the 70 wine labels on offer.

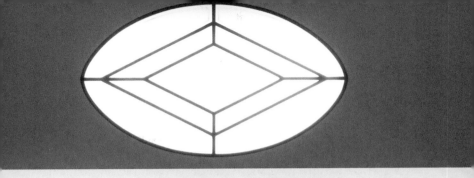

Address Via San Gregorio 46, 20124 Milan, Tel +39 026700479,
www.osteriadeltreno.it | **Getting there** Lima (M 1 red line); Stazione Centrale
(M 2 green line); Repubblica (M 3 yellow line); Regina Giovanna (tram 5, 33);
Lazzaretto (tram 1) | **Hours** Mon–Fri 12:30–2:30pm and 8pm–midnight, Sat
and Sun 8pm–midnight | **Tip** Renato Baldini started out in the fashion industry
before moving on to the flower business, and the result is his curious floral-design
shop, Mint Market – at Via Felice Casati 12 – which also has a very pleasant café
(Mon–Fri 8am–midnight, Sat–Sun 8am–2am).

63 Outlet Fashion

Great brands at low prices

Shoes, clothing, and accessories – Milan's world of fashion wants for nothing, or at least that's the impression you get walking through the streets of the city's famous high-fashion district between Via della Spiga and Via Montenapoleone. It's a virtual museum of luxury that exhibits handbags and clothes as if they were works of art. Best not to stop here though, since fashion in Milan is everywhere. It's much more fun and satisfying to go exploring, from the tiny designer shops of Via San Maurilio to the vibrant and elegant ethnic fabrics of Lisa Corti.

There are windows designed as if they were art galleries, and shops with sumptuous rooms to show off women's clothing and shoes with gravity-defying heels, as well as those with sophisticated classic or hi-tech accessories. It is a fascinating garden of fashion made of mirrors, fabric, and color. While it's fun to browse, you don't always want to break the bank. So there are two solutions: wait for the sales to come around, or head to an outlet. There are quite a few in Milan, as you would expect in the Italian capital of fashion, where people cannot sacrifice their passion for shopping even in times of austerity. But beware: you have to pick the right store.

These include Temporary in San Babila, which obviously is anything but temporary; the chain D-Magazine, which has three stores in the center of town; and the historic Il Salvagente, which opened 30 years ago and offers "made in Italy" items with discounts up to 60 percent.

Don't expert artistic window displays at these outlet stores, but you can peruse as long as you like until you find what you are looking for: a man's sweater by Roberto Cavalli, a D&G tie, a Miu Miu clutch, or a Prada skirt, for example. You'll need to find the right size, of course. But in shopping, as in everything else, a little luck goes a long way.

Address Il Salvagente, Via Fratelli Bronzetti 16, 20129 Milan; D-Magazine Outlet, Via Alessandro Manzoni 44, 20121 | Getting there Il Salvagente is in Porta Venezia (M1 red line); D-Magazine Outlet is in Montenapoleone (M3 yellow line) | Hours Il Salvagente: Mon 3–7pm, Tue–Sat 10am–7pm; D-Magazine: Outlet Sun–Mon 10am–7:30pm | Tip Lisa Corti's Indian cotton creations are very classy (Via Lecco 2, 20124, Tel +39 0220241483, www.lisacorti.com).

64__Palazzo Imperiale
When Milan was capital of the Roman Empire

In Italy the word "capital" is practically synonymous with Rome. But few people know that Milan was actually once the capital of the Western Roman Empire – from 286 to 404 AD. Even though the traces that remain cannot be compared to those of the Eternal City, the *Mediolanum* (ancient Milan) of today offers quite an interesting archaeological experience. Just follow the red dots on the pavements. Via Brisa is a good starting point, because it's where the remains of the old Palazzo Imperiale (imperial palace), built near the wall that dates from the Late Republic (147 – 30 BC), are found. The perimeter of the building was later extended by Emperor Maximianus when he decided to transfer the imperial seat to the north.

Don't be put off by the overgrown weeds and the one or two cats that have made their home among the foundations. This is all that now remains of the imperial palace, which was once equipped with an underground heating system that, when first discovered, was mistakenly believed to be a thermal bath.

In fact, the whole area was redesigned toward the end of the 3rd century to accommodate the needs of the newly installed Roman court. A hippodrome was built next to the palace, since chariot racing was a particular favorite of the Milanese. And the emperor himself would attend in person, arriving directly from the palace, in what was truly an act of political propaganda.

The circus was originally framed by two towers, and one is still visible in the courtyard of the archaeological museum, which was originally the convent of the Monastero Maggiore di San Maurizio. The tower has survived only because the architect who designed the church in the Middle Ages kept it as the bell tower.

And herein lies the rub: the Roman *Mediolanum* was literally disassembled stone by stone, marble by marble, column by column, to erect the new Christian buildings. This is all that remains.

Address Palazzo Imperiale, Via Brisa, 20123 Milan | Getting there Cairoli (M1 red line); Cadorna (M2 green line); Meravigli (tram 16, 27); Largo D'Ancona (bus 50, 58, 94) | Tip The archaeological museum, which chronicles the history of Mediolanum, is located in Corso Magenta 15. You can see ruins of the circus and of Maximinus's city walls, and visit the 3rd-century polygonal tower, adorned with 13th-century frescoes (open Tue–Sun 9am–5:30pm).

65 __ Palazzo Lombardia

The defiant skyscraper, in the shadow of the Madonnina

The construction of the Duomo by the Veneranda Fabbrica del Duomo (venerable factory of the Duomo) began at the end of the 14th century and was not considered to be officially finished until 1774, when the golden Madonnina was placed on the top of the highest spire, and was instantly adopted as the symbol of the city. At the time, the Milanese nurtured – and still do to this day – a special veneration of the "signora," so much so that it was declared that no building could be higher than the Duomo. In the 1930s this was made into law – a fact that prevented both the Branca tower of 1933 and the Velasca tower of 1958 from exceeding the fateful height of 355 feet.

Only in 1960, thanks to the unstoppable growth of modern architecture (and to a rather shrewd ploy), was the rule finally broken. The skyscraper designed for Pirelli by Giò Ponti – which the locals affectionately call the "Pirellone" – was in fact 413 feet high, and was purported to be the tallest building in Europe at the time. So as not to outdo the record height of the Madonnina, on the day of the building's opening, a copy of the statue was placed on the skyscraper's terrace. Recently, a third Madonnina was placed on the 43rd floor of Palazzo Lombardia, the 529-foot-high skyscraper that serves as the main seat of the regional government, confirming the saying that everything in Milan happens "in the shadow of the Madonnina." The building is located in the Porta Nuova District.

From the 39th floor you can enjoy a spectacular 360-degree view of the city, and with a pair of binoculars you can also see the second-highest Madonnina on the roof of the Pirellone. In fact, there are 15 Madonninas in total. One can be found among the working-class houses at Via Val Bono 2, another is on the roof of the Hebrew University in Jerusalem, and someone has even placed a Madonnina in the Himalayas.

Address The public entrance is on Piazza Città di Lombardia (at the corner with Via Francesco Restelli), 20121 Milan, Tel +39 0267651 | **Getting there** Gioia (M2 green line); Isola (M5 lilac line); Gioia/Galvani (bus 43, 60) | **Hours** Sun 10am–6pm | **Tip** At Via Melchiorre Gioia 35, at the feet of the regional government building, is the newly opened Milano Bakery, featuring an international chef and master baker. Of particular interest are the vertical gardens inside (Mon–Sat 7am–midnight, Sun 7am–6:30pm).

66 Palazzo Morando

Milan's very own history museum

After feasting your eyes on the most elegant and fashionable "Made in Italy" shop windows that line the Via della Spiga and Via Napoleone, you will reach the courtyard of Palazzo Morando – and it is like taking a step back in time. The sumptuous 16th-century palazzo, which over the centuries has hosted a number of illustrious Milanese families, was donated to the city in 1945 and opened its doors to the public as the city's museum in 1958.

Here the history and evolution of Milan are told through the paintings of the Beretta collection, an artistic journey that portrays anonymous local characters: crowds lining up for the theater, gatherings of different sorts, and city folk of all classes, including milkmen, blacksmiths, nursemaids, coachmen, and chocolatiers. You can get a feel for what it was it like to take a Sunday stroll down Corso Vittorio Emanuele in 1934, or walk along the Naviglio in the nearby Via Senato, when *el barchett* ("the ferry") sailed its waters.

You can admire the paintings in the Palazzo Morando of course, but you can also tour the 18th-century official rooms, which have been restored to their original splendor in the apartment of Morando Attendolo Bolognini, to reflect the design tastes of the time. As you walk through the corridors, you can almost imagine yourself as a guest at an 18th-century dinner party. Everything here offers a window into the place's history: the paintings, the furniture, and the decorative objects.

The Museum of Fashion and Manners opened in 2010 with a collection of more than 6,000 pieces, which are exhibited on a rotational basis, and which represent different eras, from the 18th century all the way to today's most cutting-edge designer clothes – such as the outlandish dresses of Japanese designer Issey Miyake, donated by the gallerista and Milanese art history expert Claudia Gian Ferrari.

Address Via Sant'Andrea 6, 20121 Milan | Getting there San Babila (M 1 red line), Montenapoleone (M 3 yellow line); Senato (bus 61, 94); Manzoni (tram 1) | Tip In Piazza Cavour, on the arches of Porta Nuova, you can view a marble funerary stele (1st century AD) that depicts the oldest existing representation of cloth selling. The *C. Vettius* cited in the inscription was probably a cloth merchant.

67__Parco delle Basiliche

A park with an ominous past

Just imagine if witches and warlocks could come back and liven up the Parco delle Basiliche (Basilicas' Park) with their lunatic, joyous, and liberating Sabbaths. It would be worth it if only to cancel the ignominy of the *damnatio memoriae* ("damnation of memory"), which declared that nothing should remain of the dead who received such condemnation on account of their supposed "atrocities."

A testament to this can be found in the Church of Sant'Eustorgio, where a mysterious person's name has been erased from the epithet on his/her headstone. The church, which was the seat of the Inquisition Tribunal during the Middle Ages, is located at the southern end of the Basilicas' Park, which is a park only in name and not in size.

During the day, the park is animated by young children, and retirees out for a stroll, but for those who know the fateful story of the witches it is difficult not to be touched by the place's dark past. A well-manicured lawn is not enough to erase the memories of the events of 1617, when – among the columns of the churchyard, in front of the Basilica of Saint Lawrence – Caterina de' Medici was burned at the stake for witchcraft. Today young people arrange to meet here for a beer and nothing upsets the nightlife of Porta Ticinese.

They say that the devil makes the rounds at Piazza Vetra among the syringes, broken bottles, and sprayed graffiti, despite the regular police raids. After sunset the piazza becomes a refuge for outcasts: characters that we would define "anarchic" and "hostile to social rules" – just as the emancipated women, preachers, heretics, and free spirits were labeled in the Middle Ages.

Another grim story is that of the barber Gian Giacomo Moro, unjustly accused by his pious neighbors – who would spy on him from the windows in Corso Porta Ticinese – of spreading the plague. He died on the gallows erected in the piazza in the summer of 1630.

Address Piazza Sant'Eustorgio-Via Molino delle Armi-Piazza Vetra, 20123 Milan |
Getting there Molino delle Armi / Vetra (bus 94); Ticinese / Sant'Eustorgio (bus 163) |
Tip In front of the columns of Saint Lawrence, a plaque commemorates the house of
Gian Giacomo Mora, burned down by the Inquisition Tribunal, which erected a
column on the site: the "column of infamy" with the words *damnatio aeternae* ("damned
for all eternity") engraved on it, also mentioned by Alessandro Manzoni in his famous
novel. It was dismantled in 1778, and now stands in the courtyard of the Sforza Castle.

68_Peck

The "impeckable" deli owner

The pride of Lombard gastronomy is put on display in the shop windows of Via Spadari. But long before Slow Food and all the other organizations that in recent years have contributed to the rediscovery of traditional Italian cuisine, there was Peck.

Few people remember that the classiest deli in town was opened in 1883 on Via Orefici by a merchant from Prague – the one and only Francesco Peck – with a purpose that was the total opposite of what it is today: to import culinary specialties from abroad, particularly Austro-Hungarian products such as meat, salami, smoked ham, and the heavily aromatic speck.

At first the Milanese were skeptical, but before long they all succumbed to the seduction of the new delicatessen – from the royals of the House of Savoy to the poet Gabriele D'Annunzio, who in a letter extolled "the red lobster and the fragrant truffle" as well as the sweetness of the fruits "snatched from the gardens of the Hesperides."

At the beginning of the 20th century, the store moved to its present location on Via Spadari, which merits a visit just for its fantastic Art Nouveau façade. Wrought-iron balconies frame the windows of the upstairs bar/restaurant, where you can enjoy more than 200 different kinds of infusions, teas, tisanes, and coffees. To discover the marvels of the wine cellar you have to head down to the basement.

Once upon a time, the students at the local schools would come here for sandwiches. Today, Peck is patronized only by those who are not discouraged by its exorbitant prices – the deli counter is not the only thing that reminds you of a jewelry shop. So try not to be intimidated.

The ice cream is a real treat for foodies: there are only a few flavors (including zabaglione, walnut, and chestnut), but each one is flawless. If you want to spend a bit less, try the Peck Bar on the nearby Via Cantù, where the younger set goes.

Address Store: Via Spadari 9. Bar: Via Cantù 3, 20123 Milan, Tel +39 028023161, www.peck.it | Getting there Duomo and Cordusio (M 1 red line); Duomo (M 3 yellow line) | Hours Shop: Mon 3:30–7:30pm, Tue–Sat 9:30am–7:30pm; Bar: Mon–Sat 7:30am–10pm | Tip At Via Victor Hugo 4 is Carlo Cracco's classy restaurant. Crucco is considered one of Italy's "master chefs" (2 Michelin stars) (Tel +39 02876774, www.ristorantecracco.it).

69_Piazza Gae Aulenti

Sounding the trumpets in the starchitect's square

In a country as rich in history and archaeological troves as Italy, finding somewhere to make room for new urban construction is practically impossible. But Milan did it. In just a few years, the modern skyscrapers of the Isola neighborhood, part of the wider Porta Nuova project, have radically altered the city's skyline – a fact that wouldn't raise eyebrows in most countries, but which is highly unusual for a nation as resistant to change as this one.

Piazza Gae Aulenti, a crystal-and-steel modernist behemoth, was built over the protestations of the nostalgic Milanese, who miss the old, gray neighborhood of Varesina, which bordered the Porta Garibaldi station. Covering an area of 245,000 square feet, the piazza is the collaborative effort of twenty architectural studios hailing from eight different countries.

If there is such a thing as a "21st-century historical center," this is it: on Sundays people from all over the city come here to stroll on the Via Melchiorre Gioia bridge, which connects the old Brera neighborhood to Milan's very own version of Paris's famous business district, La Défense.

The project's mastermind was an Argentinian architect named Cesar Pelli. What at first glance you might expect to be a soulless and alienating space turns out upon closer inspection to be surprisingly vital. It is filled with unexpected oddities, such as the "trumpets" on the south side of the square facing Corso Como, where a glass pane shields the entrance to escalators that lead down to the stories below. The 23 brass tubes carry all the sounds of the square to the lower levels – a modern "Ear of Dionysius" that is impossible to resist.

This playful and lighthearted square has another focal point: the foosball table area, much loved by the local youth, who seem to have ditched their video games for a more "vintage" pastime.

Address Piazza Gae Aulenti, 20124 | Getting there Gioia and Garibaldi (M 2 green line); Garibaldi (tram 33; bus 37) | Tip For a pleasant break, head over to the Feltrinelli RED (Read-Eat-Dream) cafe and bookstore, which has outdoor tables on the north side of the square. From here you can access the walkway to the 26-story award-winning Bosco Verticale (Vertical Forest) and to the UniCredit Tower, Building A of the three Pelli buildings at this location and currently the highest skyscraper in town.

70_ Platform 21
The central station's ghost train

Not all memorial sites are alike; some stay with you forever. The Shoa memorial in Milan's central station is one of these. At first glance it is little more than a concrete gallery just below the platforms. At the entrance is a large steel plaque on which the word "indifference" is engraved – a haunting reminder of the atrocities committed in this place, as well as of the injustice and inequality that still plague the world. Through the various historical documentaries screened on-site by the flocks of students who visit every year, the echo of the men, women, and children who were deported here reverberates throughout the tunnel, mixing with the rumble of the trains passing overhead.

The tunnel below Platform 21 is where hundreds of people were loaded onto convoys for a one-way trip to the concentration camps: Auschwitz, Mauthausen, even Bolzano. This area, just underneath the ordinary platforms, used to be operated by the postal service. Beginning in 1943, though, the carriages that departed from here didn't contain just mail – but human beings as well. The elevator hoist that was used to lift the "freight" train's armored carriages onto the tracks is still there today, in all its rugged and tragic desolation.

The original subterranean structure was built upon after the war, but an extensive architectural restoration undertaken by the Studio Morpurgo de Curtis stripped away the new layers and laid the tunnel bare once again. Despite the site's tragic history, the architects have succeeded in giving the place an air of humanity and reflection – of beauty, one might almost say – capable of infusing the void of in-difference with a sense of hope. Regrettably, due to lack of funds, the plans to build a library and research center are on hold for now. One can only hope that one day this place will become the open, vibrant space that the city deserves.

Address Via Ferrante Aporti (Piazza Edmond J. Safra), 20146 Milan, Tel +39 022820975, www.memorialeshoah.it | **Getting there** Stazione centrale (M 2 green line; M 3 yellow line); Luigi di Savoia (bus 90, 92); Duca d'Aosta (bus 60, 81) | **Hours** On select days (see www.facebook.com / MemorialedellaShoah) or by booking in advance (coordinamento.memoriale@memorialeshoah.it) | **Tip** On Via Ferrante Aporti (at Piazza Luigi di Savoia) sits the 1920s Art Nouveau building of the Regie Poste (Italy's old royal mail service), designed by Ulisse Stacchini, the architect of Milan's exquisite central railway station.

71 Porta Garibaldi

The graffiti station

Not long ago, Porta Garibaldi station, with its filthy walls plastered with graffiti and scrawls, was the epitome of "seedy" – and every passenger's nightmare. So, one day the association Nuova Acropoli, tired of the situation, decided to take matters into its own hands. As it happened, the association's headquarters were nearby. So a deal was struck with the local graffitists, the spray-paint rebels who regularly defaced the neighborhood's walls and who the authorities had been unable to stop. This remarkable experiment began in 2011 in the walkways beneath the station: a themed competition was announced to select the "street writers" who would decorate the underpasses.

Surprisingly, hundreds of people rushed to sign up for the competition, including many art students from the Politecnico and the Brera Academy. The first walls to receive the beauty treatment – to the surprise of the passengers getting off the trains – were the ones lining the underpass that links platforms 14 to 20 on Via Guglielmo Pepe. The theme chosen by one of the winners, Blob, was "the journey" (hence the name of the mural, *Around the World*); it depicts a couple on a bike pulling an unlikely cart full of books and curious characters.

Ento – the street name of the artistic duo comprising Federico, a cartoonist, and Cecilia, an illustrator and designer – chose to combine a number of different techniques (stencil, spray paint, acrylic) to express the world's multiplicity: a carriage full of joyous musicians in front of an old lady in a red hat.

BeLove went for a vintage look, using spray paint to sketch his own departure in a black-and-white 1920s style. All in all, almost a thousand feet of wall has been transformed into a brigade of colorful characters. The artists are all young and with a great thirst to tell their story. Just giving them a little space has made Porta Garibaldi a brighter place.

Address Stazione Porta Garibaldi, platform 20, exit on Via Guglielmo Pepe, 20124, www.escoadisola.it | Getting there Garibaldi (M2 green line; tram 33; bus 3) | Tip The project continues in the Greco Pirelli railway station with the theme *Così mi piace* ("That's the way I like it"); in the future it will include the M2 Romolo and San Cristoforo stations.

72__QC Termemilano

Relax, soak, and unwind within the Spanish walls

Porta Romana, with its onslaught of traffic and trams that trundle along the uneven tracks, is the last place in Milan where you would expect to find a spa. But there is a veritable garden of well-being right behind the Spanish walls. Built at the end of the 19th century as a tram depot, but later transformed first into a theater and then into a ballroom, the bathhouse is barely noticeable due to its modest architecture – apart from the finely wrought iron friezes. Inside, however, is a whole different story.

From the front hall, a corridor full of couples heading to and fro in white bathrobes and flip-flops leads to an elegant tearoom that serves a buffet of fruit, yogurts, and relaxing tisanes, with some extra goodies added at cocktail hour. But before partaking in such innocent indulgences (it's all very "light," after all), one should head downstairs and immerse oneself in the pleasures of ancient Rome.

Begin with the *tiepidarium* (warm baths), then move on to the *calidarium* (cold baths) and geyser pools, and top off the experience in the relaxation pool, with its rainbow of soothing colors. You'll be spoiled by all the different ways to while away the hours: from mudpacks to massages, from the Turkish baths to the Jacuzzi waterfall.

On sunny days the experience extends outdoors to the surrounding gardens, which are enclosed by the imposing walls. Here people crowd around three large pools and numerous sunbeds to absorb the rare rays of sunlight so often blocked by Milan's renowned smog. Flowerbeds of roses and aromatic plants such as bay and rosemary help to clean the air. But what's an old steam-powered tram doing parked in the middle of the lawn? Well, it's actually an eco-sauna that can reach temperatures of 158 degrees Fahrenheit. After that, it takes real nerve to dive into the outdoor 59-degree plunge pool, as good as it may be for your circulation.

Address Piazzale Medaglie d'Oro 2 (at the corner of Via Filippetti), 20135 Milan, Tel +39 0255199367, www.termemilano.com | **Getting there** Porta Romana (M 3 yellow line; tram 9; bus 62, 77) | **Hours** Mon–Thu 9:30am–11pm, Fri 9:30–12:30am, Sat and Sun 8:30–12:30am with buffet breakfast | **Tip** Porta Romana was one of the six main gateways along the perimeter of the walls, which, seen from above, are shaped like a heart, with this gate at the tip. According to legend the *porta* was erected by Philip III of Spain to honor the arrival of his future bride, Margaret of Austria (in 1596).

73__Reminders of War

The air-raid shelter of Porta Lodovica

During World War II, the Allies' bombs pummeled the city of Milan. The older generation still remembers the wail of the sirens that would send everyone scattering in panic, and emptied the streets in seconds. The silence was soon followed by the deafening sound of exploding bombs, breaking glass and collapsing masonry. And when it was all over, the smell of smoke, and then the dust. But as long as no one had been injured, that was what mattered.

Throughout the city there are many reminders of those tragic events. One, for example, is found on the wall of a building in Porta Lodovica. Here, at number 2, you can still make out the initials U.S. next to a white arrow pointing downward. Contrary to what you might think, they don't stand for "United States," rather they indicate an emergency exit (*uscita di sicurezza* in Italian).

The same goes for the big R (standing for the Italian word *rifugio*, which means "shelter") on a painted white wall near a modern pharmacy.

Following Mussolini's speech on June 10th, 1940, in which he announced that Italy was entering the war, those symbols came to represent the difference between life and death to many Milanese.

Milan's city council set up at least a hundred air-raid shelters around the city, using cellars, warehouses, and underground tunnels, and then, of course, you had the DIY shelters that families and residents in apartment blocks organized by themselves. These shelters were not always supplied with anti-bomb and anti-gas equipment, but it was important to be able to identify the entrance or escape routes in the shortest possible time (i.e., a few seconds). This is what the black-and-white arrows were for.

Today people hardly notice them, and fortunately, they are no longer needed. To find them you just have to look closely. Unless of course a building has been repainted in the last 75 years.

Address Piazzale Porta Lodovica 2, 20136 Milan | Getting there Corso Italia / S. Sofia
(tram 15 and bus 94) | Tip The air-raid shelters were positioned in different parts of
the city: in Piazza Cinque Giornate under the monument to the revolutionary
movements of 1848; under the monument in Piazza Giuseppe Garibaldi; and in the
barracks on Via Riccardo Pitteri where still today you can see the conical cement
towers sticking up from the ground, whose shape was supposed to deviate the trajectory
of the bombs.

74_Rotonda della Besana

A children's colosseum in the old cemetery

Milan is a strange place. Suffice to say that some of the city's most architecturally significant buildings are found in cemeteries. An example is the Rotonda della Besana: built at the beginning of the 18th century as the *foppone* (literally "large pit" – i.e., cemetery) of the nearby Ospedale Maggiore – this elliptical colonnade, which encircles the piazza surrounding the San Michele ai Sepolcri Nuovi church, is a veritable masterpiece of elegance and proportion.

From the outside it looks like a Roman amphitheater with a perimeter of flat bricks. But if it were possible to view it from above, it would be instantly apparent that the structure is not round but quadrilateral.

Inside the colonnade a succession of columns and arches spans the perimeter: a truly breathtaking sight. You'd be forgiven for wondering if this is the work of Bramante, or of some other great architect of the time. But you'd be wrong: the building dates back to the late Baroque period and was designed by the architects Attilio Arrigoni and Francesco Croce as a cemetery for the poor, then subsequently transformed by Napoleon into barracks, a barn, stables, a hospice, and a warehouse.

The Rotunda was finally returned to the city in 1940, and today houses the MUBA, a museum-workshop for children that is open to anyone who seeks a bit of peace within the walls. Inside there is a cafe, a bistro, and a bookshop where you can find educational books for kids. There are a number of activities to choose from: design and storytelling workshops, memory boxes, and experimental theater.

Browsing through the boxes on the shelves you will find an almost endless selection of materials – beads, glues, cardboard, scraps of metal, wood, and fabrics – with which to create your own collages. So challenge your creativity and let your inner child run amok with auditory stimuli, color associations, waste recycling, and much more.

Address Via Enrico Besana 12, 20123 Milan, Tel +39 0243980402, www.muba.it |
Getting there Monte Nero / Spartaco (tram 9); Corso Porta Vittoria / Camera del
Lavoro (tram 12, 23, 27 and bus 60, 73); Besana (bus 77–84) | Hours Mon
9:30am–3:30pm, Tue–Fri 9:30am–6:30pm, Sat and Sun 10am–7pm (consult the
website for workshops) | Tip At Piazza Cinque Giornate 4 is the historic Gelateria
Umberto, one of Milan's best ice-cream parlors. There may only be a few flavors,
but they are very high quality. If it's not too crowded you might even find a seat
(Tue–Sun 2–11pm).

75_ Sadler & Sadlerino
Good food for all

Michelin stars and Gambero Rosso cutlery can tend to alienate rather than to draw people to restaurants, especially in times of austerity. A terrible mistake, if you ask Claudio Sadler, the creative and affable Milanese chef who runs this prestigious eatery on the Naviglio.

The restaurant is divided into two distinct sections, both of which have been carefully designed, down to the smallest detail. One, Ristorante Sadler, encompasses lush VIP rooms and discreet and lovely romantic niches. The tables here are decorated with designer porcelain and crystal glasses for savoring wine. An added stroke of genius: the dishes are served in geometric compositions akin to culinary works of art – so much so that it's a shame to have to spoil them with a fork. But they're so mouth-wateringly delicious that putting up any resistance is futile.

Then there is Chic 'n Quick – or the "Sadlerino," as it is affectionately called by diners in the know, a fast food *trattoria* that looks out onto the street. At lunchtime it is busy with customers delighted to order from a menu that the chef has prepared with his usual rigor and flair for creativity. The price? Twenty euros for a two-course meal and a dessert (excluding drinks).

In any uninspired bar in the center of Milan, this is what you might pay for a plate of microwaved pasta and a mixed salad with canned corn. But "Da Sadler" is no ordinary place; it is an exercise in gastronomic socialism. This is an experiment that is part of a wider revolution in the world of haute cuisine, aimed at ensuring that good food is no longer just for the elite.

Anyone who is interested in learning what goes on behind the scenes may join one of the many evening events here, where participants can cook their meals along with the chef.

And no false pride, please: Claudio Sadler has even collaborated with McDonald's.

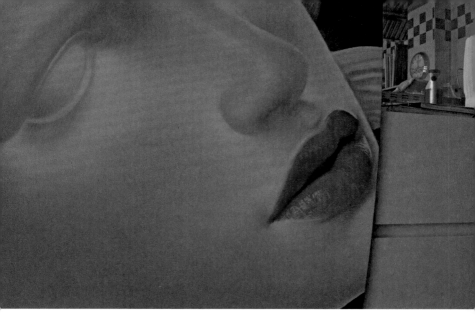

Address Via Ascanio Sforza 77, 20141 Milan, Tel +39 0258104451 (Ristorante Sadler), +39 0289503222 (Chic 'n Quick), www.sadler.it | **Getting there** Romolo (M2 green line + bus 91); Liguria (bus 51, 91); Nav. Pavese/Rimini (bus 59) | **Hours** Sadler: Mon–Sat 7:30–11pm; Chic 'n Quick: Tue–Sat 12:30–2:30pm/ 7:30–10:30pm, Mon 7:30–10:30pm | **Tip** At number 47 there is a small, lively venue with tables on the sidewalk, owned by a surfer and an Australian. If you're interested in tasting an aboriginal burger, Burger Wave is the place for you.

76__Saint Christopher on the Naviglio

First stop on the way to Santiago de Compostela

Saint Christopher on the Naviglio has not lost his vocation as protector of wayfarers. The tradition continues today, attested to by the many pilgrims who come here to get the *credenziali* ("credentials," also known as the pilgrim's passport) before embarking on the pilgrimage to Santiago de Compostela. Situated along the route from the countryside of Lomellina to the city, next to the old bridge crossing the river, the church is immersed in a nearly rural landscape and is beloved by young couples who come here to marry. It boasts a history almost as important as the frescoes that decorate its interior.

Originally, this was a simple chapel with a typical bell-shaped roof. The church was added only at the end of the 13th century, and the pilgrim's hostel a century later. From the piazza you can make out the entrances to two adjacent chapels. The oldest one, on the left, is recognizable by its beautiful 15th-century door with a delicately worked Gothic terra-cotta rosette in the middle. The one on the right is known as the Cappella Ducale (Ducal Chapel) and was built at the beginning of the 15th century by Gian Galeazzo Visconti. Above, next to the emblem of Milan with the cross, is the symbol of the noble family, with its characteristic snake (which appears to be devouring a human but it is actually giving birth to it). There are still a few traces of the polychrome frescoes that once adorned both façades.

A recently restored Byzantine-influenced Christ Blessing (dating back to the late 12th century) can be seen on the left side of the apse vault in the oldest part of the nave. There are several precious wooden statues, among them a Saint Christopher from the 14th century and one from the 16th century, which testifies to the locals' devotion to this patron saint of travelers. The Milanese still like to meet here, especially the Sunday cyclists who come to pedal along the Naviglio.

Address Via San Cristoforo 3, Alzaia Naviglio Grande, 20144 Milan,
Tel +39 0248951413, www.chiesasancristoforo.it | **Getting there** Ludovico il Moro /
Pestalozzi (tram 2 and bus 324, 325, 329, 351); Ponte delle Milizie (bus 90, 91) | **Hours**
Mon – Sun 9am – 12pm/3:30 – 7pm | **Tip** Nearby, the Circolo Canottieri San Cristoforo
serves coffee, has an open-air restaurant, and provides canoeing on the Naviglio even to
nonmembers (Alzaia Naviglio Grande 122, www.canottierisancristoforo.it).

77__San Bernardino
The house of bones

Maybe it was the custom of the time, or simply the ingenuity of the ossuary custodian, but the fact of the matter was that something had to be done with all those bones from the cemetery of the nearby leper hospital. It was therefore decided to use the wall niches as frames for a rather macabre picture, with human tibias used as an added refinement, their linearity lending itself magnificently to the bizarre creation.

So that was how things went. In 1430, the cemetery chapel was given to the Milan-based Disciplini (disciplinarians) confraternity, whose patron was Saint Bernardino of Siena. Following a series of restorations in the 17th and 18th centuries, it was transformed into a much larger church, connected to the first by a triumphal arch. From here a corridor leads to the ossuary.

As people died – many of them due to the plague – the "house of bones," as the populace knew it, began to fill up with the skeletons of sick and poor people, of prisoners and murder victims, and even of a few nobles who couldn't find a more dignified burial place. The cult of the ossuary grew in popularity over time, and perhaps also for this reason, when the place underwent restoration, it was decided to give the site a complete makeover.

Tibias, femurs, and skulls were divided up and arranged in an orderly fashion inside the gold-stuccoed framed niches. Today, two columns of skulls flank the statue of Our Lady of Sorrows, with the dying Christ at her feet, above the altar, surrounded by friezes of tibias that look like angels' trumpets and ex-votos.

The frescoed ceiling of the cupola, painted by the Venetian artist Sebastiano Ricci, dominates from above, depicting the triumph of the souls ascending into paradise. It is surrounded by skulls that seem to stare as they protrude like pigeons from the cornice above the oblivious visitor.

Address Piazza Santo Stefano/Via Verziere 2, 20122 Milan | Getting there Duomo and San Babila (M1 red line); Duomo (M3 yellow line); Larga (tram 15); Sforza/Andreani (77,94) | Hours Mon–Fri 7:30am–12pm, Sat 7:30am–12:30pm | Tip At Via Larga 2, the Neapolitan Gran Caffè Cimmino is a great place to have breakfast. Its custard brioches and ricotta-filled puff pastries are truly delicious, especially if accompanied by a cappuccino (Mon–Sun 6:30am–8pm).

78__San Maurizio al Monastero

The "Sistine Chapel" of Milan

Forced into a cloistered life, the erudite nuns of the Benedictine convent of San Maurizio would cheer themselves up by traveling vicariously among the magnificent scenes frescoed on the interior walls of the church. Upon entering, it becomes immediately apparent why this is known as the Sistine Chapel of Milan. In fact, the *Last Supper* by Leonardo da Vinci is not far away (the master was at the time commissioned to paint the *Virgin of the Rocks*).

The convent of San Maurizio rounded up the best artists of the Lombard School, including Bernardino Luini, to decorate its church. This is not surprising, given that the convent's sponsors included Ippolita Sforza, niece of the Duke of Milan Ludovico Moro and wife of Alessandro Bentivoglio, a nobleman from Bologna and nephew of Alessandro Sforza, who had confined four of her daughters to the convent. What is surprising is not to find crowds lined up at the entrance to this magnificent example of Renaissance painting. Entirely painted in tempera, the colorful frescoes depict numerous biblical scenes, rural landscapes, episodes relating to the history of the Church, and powerful people belonging to the family of the abbess.

Many daughters from the most aristocratic families of the time were enclosed in this golden cage, which communicated with the outside world through a grille in the wall. The church was built with a single nave, divided in the middle by a painted partition that didn't reach the ceiling so that the nuns could attend mass without the risk of seeing outside or of being seen. Vice versa, from the outside one could only hear the polyphonic chants of the female voices of the choir, accompanied by the pipe organ made by Antegnati, also from the 16th century. It's a cloistered destiny that seems to continue to this day, seeing that many ignore the beauty hidden behind the wall.

Address Corso Magenta 13, 20123 Milan | **Getting there** Cordusio and Cairoli (M1 red line); Cadorna (M2 green line); Meravigli (tram 16, 27); Largo D'Ancona (bus 50, 58, 94) | **Hours** Tue–Sun 9:30am–5:30pm | **Tip** In front of the church is the beautiful façade of the Baroque-style Palazzo Litta, built in the second half of the 17th century by Francesco Maria Richini for Count Bartolomeo Aresa, one of the most influential men in Milan. Inside there are a series of courtyards and a sumptuous grand staircase that leads to a *piano nobile* ("noble floor"), where the national railway company now has its offices.

79 _ Sant'Ambroeus
The Belle Époque cake shop

The exquisite delicacies of the Belle Époque come to life among the large Murano glass lampshades, silver mirrors, and wood paneling of the cafe Sant'Ambroeus. Behind the glass panes, assorted chocolate pralines, confetti, and mini cakes line the counters like little jewels. And as soon as you cross the porticos and enter the shop, the delicious aroma of Arabic coffee tickles the nostrils, like incense in a church.

You have entered a temple of micro-patisserie, and it's just around the corner from the Teatro La Scala and the Galleria Vittorio Emanuele. It all began in 1936, thanks to two master bakers who had fine-tuned their culinary art in the restaurants of Paris, but looked to Vienna as an educational point of reference for chocolate.

The Milan of the 1930s was fashionable and full of life, irony, and taste, and the Milanese had a great passion for desserts, cream-filled cakes, custards, and apple strudels. At the time, it was common for the lady of the house to send a servant to purchase the biscuits that she would then serve in her drawing room at teatime.

Today the occasion is more likely to be a private party, a gala dinner, or a work lunch in style, but other than that, not much has changed. At lunchtime, the shop fills up with customers from the nearby high towers of finance, fashion, and communications.

And everyone, even the shop assistant from across the road, can afford to pay an extra 10 cents for a coffee – and it's worth it. Moreover, it comes with a homemade chocolate sweet included in the price.

At Christmastime it is worth stopping by just to get a whiff of the scent of freshly baked – and utterly prodigious – *panettone* (a type of sweet bread loaf). Milan's culinary symbol can be sent to any household in the world within 48 hours, reads a sign hanging on the wall. But to taste it here is another thing altogether.

Address Corso Giacomo Matteotti 7, 20121 Milan, Tel +39 0276000540 | **Getting there** Colonne San Lorenzo (bus 94); Piazza Resistenza Partigiana (tram 2, 14) | **Hours** Mon–Sat 7:45am–8:30pm | **Tip** At Via Montenapoleone 8 (at Via Sant'Andrea) is Cova, another historical cake and sweet shop, founded in 1817 by one of Napoleon's soldiers. Its products are so well known that they are copied just like haute couture designer brands; though its imitators come nothing close to the real thing (Mon–Sat 7:45am–8:30pm).

80_ Santa Maria alla Fontana

The miracle of the holy water

The entrance to Santa Maria alla Fontana is free, but getting a miracle costs one and a half euros (unless the price has gone up). For this small sum, the faithful receive a plastic cup with which to quench their thirst. According to tradition, Charles II d'Amboise, governor of Milan in the early 16th century, drank from the fountain and was miraculously cured of an eye infection. The history of the healing spring, which flows straight out of the rock, begins with the building of the sanctuary above the *sacellum* (small shrine), where the source was found.

Looking at the façade of the neo-Renaissance-style church, on the right is a staircase that descends to a chapel where water gushes out of 11 copper spouts into a basin. This underground area looks onto a cloister so elegant in its classical proportions that until 1982, when an archivist discovered a contract dated March 17, 1508, assigning the project to the architect Giovanni Antonio Amedeo, it was believed to have been designed by Bramante, who was known to be working in Milan at the time. The 16th-century frescoes have been attributed to the painter Bernardino Luini's workshop; the 17th-century lunettes that decorate the arches are also of particular interest.

Whether it was because of the popular belief in the water's miraculous powers or whether it was due to the fact that clean water was not easy to come by at the time, the sanctuary performed an important sanitary function over the centuries, especially during the plague.

Despite the legend, however, the holy fountain was ultimately unable to save Charles II d'Amboise. What he mistook for a cure turned out to simply be a temporary reprieve. He died four years later, at the age of thirty-eight.

The holy water that once sprung from an underground rock today flows from the taps of Milan's civic aqueduct. But it doesn't hurt to have a little faith.

Address Via Thaon di Revel 28, 20159 Milan | **Getting there** Zara (M 3 yellow line); Stelvio / Farini (bus 90, 92) | **Hours** Mon – Sun 8:30am – 12pm and 3:30 – 5:30pm | **Tip** At Via Thaon di Revel 9 is the Spanish locale Ajoblanco, famous for its tapas, served in 50 different varieties to enjoy at the wooden tables, as tradition decrees (Tue – Sun 6pm – 2am, Tel +39 026686577).

81 Santa Maria della Passione

The solemn music of the twin organs

It's always awe-inspiring to enter the basilica during Vespers, as the wooden doors close behind you and the church, which dates back to the late Renaissance, is enveloped in semi-darkness. As the singing of the evening prayers echoes off the walls of the nave, the notes of the organ remind us that this devotion – a cry from the soul – goes all the way back to the origins of Christianity.

Normally, in a Benedictine monastery, the life of the monks is charted by the Liturgy of the Hours: even today, when the chants take flight in a church like Santa Maria della Passione – second only to the Duomo in size – time comes to a halt and cultural differences are swept aside by the sheer power of the music. This is the magic of the organ – or rather of the "twin organs" that have a long tradition in this church. The oldest of the two organs dates back to the second half of the 16th century. Then, in the 17th century, the decision was made to add another, twin instrument left of the transit, in order to add solemnity to the choir's music. The work was commissioned to Gian Giacomo Antegnati, who had also built the Duomo's organ.

The first organ, located *in cornu Epistolae* (right of the altar where the gospel is read), still has the original wind chest, while the internal instrument was replaced in 2001 by the Mascioni company with one that has two keyboards comprising 56 notes and a 30-note pedal board suitable for Baroque music.

The second 17th-century organ, located in the choir, has had its sound box restored. So after three centuries the pair of organs has returned to play in unison – or rather, to converse with each other – while the nearby cloister, where the monks used to live, now houses the Giuseppe Verdi conservatory, with its impressive library and collection of antique stringed instruments.

Address Via Conservatorio 14, 20122 Milan, www.lacappellamusicale.com | **Getting there** San Babila (M1 red line); Monforte/Donizetti (bus 54, 61); Modrone (94) | **Hours** Organ Vespers from Oct–June, every 2nd Sun of the month at 4:30pm | **Tip** In the side street, on Via Vincenzo Bellini, stop and admire the house of the architect Alfredo Campanini, built between 1904 and 1906. It is one of the best examples of Milanese Art Nouveau style.

82 — Santa Maria la Rossa

Proud to be an abbess

A church, a number of farmhouses, a public library, and Mrs. Carla's cafe: this is where the inhabitants of this little suburb on the banks of the Naviglio Grande come to chat, read, or simply while away the hours under the bar's wooden and brick canopy. This is also where the members of the local G.A.S. groups (*gruppo di acquisto solidale*, which is Italian for "ethical purchasing groups," an Italian-based system for purchasing goods collectively) meet to pick up their crates of freshly picked organic produce.

The church, called Santa Maria la Rossa (Mary the Red), probably because of the color of its bricks, is clearly ancient, though the exact date of its foundation is unknown. Historians consider this an example of open-air stratigraphy (a branch of geology that studies rock layers and layering) dating back to Roman times, as indicated by the 2nd-century mosaics found inside a building unearthed during the excavations.

The cross-shaped *sacellum* (small shrine), visible under the glass floor inside the church is believed to be from the 4th to the 6th century. Further additions and transformations were implemented during the Carolingian period (8th to 9th centuries), with the church receiving its final makeover during the Romanesque period (10th century).

The abbesses of the Benedictine order lived in the convent, and some of them are mentioned in testimonial writings: Donna Bontà (1148), Donna Cecilia (1173), and Donna Agata (1198). Among the many distinguished female guests was Maria de Robacarri – who promoted important restoration work in the 14th century both to the structure and the frescoes, and to whom a headstone is dedicated. This was around the time that the initial section of the Naviglio, connecting Milan to Pavia, was built, so that in 1455 the wedding procession of Tristano Sforza and Beatrice d'Este could pass through here and pay a visit to "Santa Maria Ruffa."

Address Via Chiesa Rossa, entrance in Via San Domenico Savio, Alzaia Naviglio Pavese, 20142 Milan | **Getting there** Abbiategrasso (M 2 green line; tram 15); Savio (tram 79) | **Hours** The church is open for mass. The library is open Mon–Fri 9am–3pm, Wed 3–7pm, Sat 10am–6pm | **Tip** About a quarter mile south on the Naviglio is the Conca Fallata ("faulty basin"), so called because of its unfortunate vicissitudes: the construction of the basin, which was supposed to facilitate navigation to Pavia, began in the 16th century but was completed only in 1819.

83 Santa Maria Presso San Satiro

Bramante's trick: the apse that isn't there

A church without an apse must have been unimaginable to the young Donato Bramante, already one of the best architects of his time. He was by then in Milan, at the end of the 15th century, when Galeazzo Maria Sforza, duke of the city, commissioned him to build a church. The only problem was that the chosen site was exceptionally small, and it already contained a 9th-century *sacellum* dedicated to Saint Satyrus – who was not just any old saint but the brother of Saint Ambrose, patron saint of the city. So this was already an important place. As if that wasn't enough, a miracle had also occurred here in 1241: an unbalanced young man had attacked with a dagger (still preserved) the fresco of a Madonna and Child, and the wound had started to bleed.

As the shrine became the object of growing devotion, the duke decided that it was time to build a bigger church. The only problem was that the surrounding buildings limited the space available for new construction. So Bramante, assisted by his colleagues, threw caution to the wind and designed a plan with three naves. The width of the central nave was to be equal to the two wings of the transept, surmounted by a vaulted ceiling inlaid with polychrome coffers, a nod to the basilica of Saint Andrew designed by Leon Battista Alberti.

The result is rather remarkable, almost on a par with a "normal" basilica. By resorting to all the available studies on perspective (and by taking a few risks), Bramante managed to design an apse behind the altar with a depth of only 40 inches, resulting in an eye-catching vista. Today the *trompe-l'œil* effect is perfect, with the horizontal lines making it possible to view the cupola from any angle. In the lower part, a fake choir painted on stucco supports the structure of this ingenious deceit.

Address Via Torino 17, 20123 Milan | Getting there Duomo (M1 red line, M3 yellow line); Orefici (tram 2, 12, 14, 16, 27) | Hours Tue–Sat 9:30am–5:30pm Sun 2–5:30pm | Tip Behind the church (coming from Via Mazzini) one gets a fine view of the Romanesque tower (10th century), one of the oldest in the city, and of the octagonal baptistery, also designed by Bramante, which contains some beautiful terra-cotta friezes.

84_ Santeria

Brunch and coworking: the world in a courtyard

On the edge of the suburbs but close enough to the Politecnico – the university of science and technology – the vaguely hipster-ish Santeria has become a focal point for the young and eclectic geniuses who gravitate to the school. They come here for Sunday brunch and to give their brains a rest from numbers and algorithms. The open-air courtyard, where the students sit at colorful tables, is the heart of this micro-world in constant evolution.

The place is a veritable trove of oddities and curiosities: beginning with the "emotional shop," where you can find unusual books, listen to vinyl records, take part in readings, buy unconventional designer clothes from Berlin (Ucon Acrobatics and Wemoto Clothing), London (Supremebeing), or Sydney (Rhythm), or support emerging designers who artfully mix organic clothing, street-ware, and sustainable fashion, and encourage the idea that "small is beautiful."

Here, ideas, projects, and opportunities don't just come together at happy hour but are conceived during the day at the desks of the shared work spaces, where, for a fairly low price, you can use the locale's computers, printers, boardrooms, and anything else that you may need to organize your work.

The three-story building has many people coming and going – from music bands rehearsing for a concert to photographers, from design teams to lone freelancers.

Anyone can create an event or participate in one of the many initiatives, which include marketing, management, and communications courses. Some just want to get out of the house for a coffee, bringing along their tablets to hook up to the free Wi-Fi network; others stop by for a home cooked meal. All that is needed is a little patience, as the dishes aren't premade but prepared on the spot. There's no risk of getting bored, though: there is always someone to talk to while you wait.

Address Via Privata Ettore Paladini 8, 20133 Milan, Tel + 39 0236798121, www.santeriamilano.it | **Getting there** Don San Martino/Marescalchi (bus 54); Amedeo/Paladini (tram 5) | **Hours** Bar: Tue–Sun 11am–10:30pm. Restaurant: Tue–Sun 12:30pm–10pm (brunch Sat and Sun only, reservations are preferred) | **Tip** Wine and chocolate in a variety of combinations is what the Enoteca Diapason at Via Lomellina 48 offers. It also organizes themed events, tasting courses, and meetings with food producers (Mon 3:30–7:30pm, Tue–Sat 10am–1pm/3:30–7:30pm).

85_ Scimmie
Jazz on the Navigli

This legendary live music club has aged well, and remains a focal point of the Navigli nightlife. It first opened its doors on June 6th, 1981, with Karl Berger playing piano and Attilio Zanchi on double bass, with the aim of "bringing music out of the basements." The venue – founded by Sergio Israel, who still runs it with his wife, Monica – started out as a club for jazz enthusiasts. Musicians the likes of the trumpeter Enrico Rava were regulars here.

As the clientele – more or less always the same, hence the familiar atmosphere – sipped wine and smoked (back then it was still allowed), percussionists and singers would improvise on Scimmie's stage.

It was not long before the place became *the* cult venue for live music, or, in other words, a trial by fire for anyone who wanted to make a name for themselves. Thanks to Sergio's instinct for discovering new talent, some of the best names in music played their first notes here, from Enzo Jannacci to Elio e Le Storie Tese. To perform here, in other words, meant that you had made it. Over the years jazz, blues, rock, and even cabaret acts (for a while) took turns on this stage.

Countless artists have made the speakers vibrate with their gritty voices, scintillating guitars, and bruised keyboards. Just look at the posters on the walls: Andy Summers, the multi-instrumentalist from the Police; jazz saxophonist Steve Lacy; young Italian singer/song-writer Malika Ayane, to name a few. But why talk of the past? The venue hasn't changed much, after all. The original signpost – "Man is more of an ape than any of the apes," a quote from Nietzsche – is still there, as well as the old counter and the timeless rum cocktails.

A band is performing onstage almost every evening, and you can still feel the music beat through the walls covered with autographs of the many great musicians who have passed through here.

Address Via Ascanio Sforza 49, 2013 Milan, Tel +39 0239811039, www.scimmie.it |
Getting there Transit Romolo (M2 green line); Liguria (bus 91); XXIV Maggio
(tram 3) | Hours Tue–Sun 8pm–2am | Tip Nearby, at Via Conchetta 20, is a bizarre
bohemian bar called Farmacia Alcolica (Alcoholic Pharmacy), fitted out just like an old
pharmacy: retro atmosphere, crystal lampshades, cuckoo clocks, and marble counter
(Tel +39 3394179159).

86 Scior Carera

The voice of the people

Pretty much every Italian city had a Roman bust where the populace could leave anonymous messages of protest, complaints, mottoes, and ironic gibes (usually political in nature) aimed at whoever happened to be in power at the time. In Rome it is called *Pasquino*, in Milan *El Scior Carera* (Mr. Carera), but it's basically the same thing.

In the crowded portico near Zara, the virile statue, dating back to the 3rd century, is barely noticeable, leaning against the entrance of number 13 almost as if he were the doorman of the elegant building. Clad in a toga, motionless, and silent, Mr. Carera, or "the stone man," is the most knowledgeable witness of what goes on in the vicinity.

The epigraph on the base of the bust reads: *Carere debet omni vitio, qui in alterum dicere paratus est* ("Anybody who wants to criticize someone should be free from all faults"). But ordinary citizens didn't know Latin and thought Carere was the character's name. Whoever the statue represents or where it was originally located, no one knows.

It has been moved several times, and over the centuries its face has been modified. Roman sculptures were in fact made up of different pieces: the head was usually made by a specialist artisan and then joined to the other parts. In the Middle Ages it was thought best to replace the original effigy (now lost), which probably represented an important Roman magistrate of Cicero's time, with that of the archbishop Adelmanno Menclozzi.

However, this is nothing compared to what happened in 1848, during the Five Days of Milan, when the Milanese rebelled against Austria and turned the city upside down. It was then that Mr. Carera became a moral symbol for the people, and took on the role of spokesperson for the rioters: every day the people would leave messages at the statue's feet calling for justice and freedom.

Address Corso Vittorio Emanuele 13, 20122 Milan | **Getting there** Duomo and San Babila (M 1 red line, M 3 yellow line); San Babila (bus 54, 61); Durini (60 – 73) | **Tip** At Via Santa Radegonda 16, a visit to Luini Panzerotti's esteemed delicatessen, founded in 1888, is a must. It's worth lining up for one of its famous hot, filled *panzerottis* (small calzones), perfect for a midday snack (Mon 10am – 3pm, Tue – Sat 10am – 8pm).

CARERE·DEBET·OMNI·VITIO·QVI
IN·ALTERVM·DICERE·PARATVS·EST

87__Sforza Castle

A breathtaking view from the battlements

The "wall-walks" are the most interesting feature of medieval fortifications like this one, as they immediately conjure visions of the memorable seizes we have so often seen in the movies. The battlements of the Sforza Castle – a maze of dimly lit passageways that connect the various watchtowers – are the archetype of such wall-walks, which are as much a part of Italian history as they are of our collective imagination.

The castle has a mysterious fascination that takes visitors back in time. Built in the mid-15th century by Duke Francesco Sforza, this fortress has a troubled history. Napoleon caused quite a lot of damage to it, housing his army here for a time and showing no regard for the beautifully frescoed halls, which he used as stables for his troops' horses. The rest was left to an Austrian garrison that stationed one of its headquarters in the castle. The Milanese were so angry with the intruders that they sacked the castle during the "Five Days of Milan" revolt in 1848.

What you see today is a reconstruction of the original structure, built after the Unification of Italy in 1861 under the direction of architect Luca Beltrami. It was only in 1905 that the Filarete Tower was finished, in the castle's original 15th-century Gothic-Renaissance style. It was an endeavor the Milanese were determined to complete, since to them the castle is a symbol of the ancient Duchy and its independence.

Today the battlements offer visitors an impressive view of the city and the Duomo. Looking north, the beautiful snow-capped skyline of the Alps is dominated by the Monte Rosa; and looking down on the Ghirlanda ("covered road"), one can relive stories of intrigue, escape, and passionate encounters. From here, a messenger could escape unseen during an attack. It is said that one secret passageway led all the way to Villa Simonetta, outside the city walls.

Address Piazza Castello, 20121 Milan | **Getting there** Cairoli (M 1 red line); Cadorna (M 2 green line); Cairoli (tram 1; bus 50, 61) | **Hours** Castle: Mon–Sun 7am–6pm (winter), 7am–7pm (summer); to walk the battlements and the Ghirlanda you must book in advance (Ad Artem, Tel +39 026596937) | **Tip** In the Corte Ducale there is a stone engraving from the "Column of Infamy" wrongly accusing the barber Gian Giacomo Mora of being a plague spreader during the Great Plague of Milan. He was executed by the Inquisition in 1630. Alessandro Manzoni makes a reference to the episode in the *Promessi Sposi*.

88_ The Steam Factory
A cultural center for the arts

Among Milan's institutions, the most effervescent is the Fabbrica del Vapore ("The Steam Factory"). It is a bubbling pot of initiatives, meetings, and happenings of all kinds, situated in a disused industrial area, the old working-to-middle-class Procaccini District, which was once located on the outskirts of town but is today a stone's throw from the city center, just outside the "limited traffic zone." It is an area that has resisted Milan's steady gentrification, as attested to by the many graffiti-covered apartment buildings, which haven't yet been transformed into yuppie offices.

Up until 1936, this is where the components for trams and trains were built. In front of the painted gate that leads to the Factory's large courtyard, the old tram tracks still protrude from the uneven porphyry paving stones, a treacherous spot for cyclists and scooters.

The workers used to call the building where the cars were assembled "the Cathedral." Today, it is an exhibition hall. Particularly impressive is the open-air piazza – spanning 130,000 square feet – where packed concerts and shows are held in the summer. All around are the various warehouses, now transformed into 14 eclectic cultural laboratories.

The (nonprofit) vocation of the association is to stimulate the experimentation and blending of diverse art forms: among these, photography, music, theater, dance, cabaret, design, and creative writing. One's imagination is truly the only limit here. It is a creative work in progress, but far from unsophisticated.

Among the residents is the Studio Azzurro group, famous for its highly emotive video installations and well established on the Italian and European theatrical scene. You don't have to sign up for a work-shop or an event to appreciate the Factory – there is always something to see, an artist to meet, and new creative relationships to forge.

Address Via Giulio Cesare Procaccini 4, 20154 Milan, Tel +39 3929965885, www.fdvlab.org | Getting there Garibaldi (M 2 green line); Procaccini (tram 2; bus 37) | Hours Check the website for links to the individual events, exhibitions, and workshops. | Tip At Via Procaccini 38, there is the Casalinghi Outlet, which sells everything for the home: plates, pans, and small household appliances at reduced prices, while at number 32, there is the Bassetti Outlet, a household name for home textiles (towels, sheets, etc.).

89 __ Streets of Art Nouveau

The artistic façades of the new century

The *Novecento* ("new century") refers to the 20th century – when economic power passed to the emerging middle class of entrepreneurs and industrial families. This marked the beginning of a fresh chapter in the country's history, and of Milan's rise as the capital of Italian finance. Irreverent and avant-garde, this new class challenged tradition by erecting imaginative, eclectic, and bizarre – not to mention overly decorated – new residences in the heart of the old city.

The façades between Via Malpighi and Via Sirtori, in the Porta Venezia area, are a perfect example, inlaid with floral friezes, polychrome majolica tiles, wrought iron, and reliefs of all kinds. Setting the trend were architects like Giuseppe Sommaruga and Giovan Battista Bossi, assisted by an army of artisans in competition with one another to bring to life, in the most imaginative way, this new aesthetic lingo, called Art Nouveau. All rules were cast aside, and for the first time neoclassical forms were combined with Baroque eccentricity and modern rationality. The iconography abounds in naturalistic panoramas and rural traits.

Walking along Casa Galimberti you get a distinct feeling of not being alone, as every window is flanked by elegant male and female figures watching the street amid a flurry of trees and grapevines. Such bold provocations were common for this new entrepreneurial class that had no qualms about taking on tradition, and who took inspiration from the Art Nouveau movement: its irreverence and unruliness, but also its unconventional style and use of innovative materials such as cement and wrought iron.

The World Expo of 1906 became a chance for the city to show off its new spirit: forward-looking and worldly but also vain and ostentatious. Charting the rise of the nouveau riche, colors, decorations, and sculptures began brightening the neighborhoods. Today, they still keep the passersby company.

Address Via Marcello Malpighi 3, 20129 Milan, www.duomomilano.it | Getting there Porta Venezia (M1 red line; tram 3); Oberdan (tram 9) | Tip At Via Paolo Frisi 2 at Via Melzo is the Biblioteca Comunale Venezia, located inside an Art Nouveau building that once housed the city's first cinema, opened in 1910.

90_ Studio Castiglioni
The household atelier of the designer brothers

Designer brothers Achille and Pier Giacomo Castiglioni literally changed the interiors of Italy's homes with their simple, colorful, and ingenious kitchen utensils and home décor.

"Aesthetics was never an affectation for my father, more than anything else he was interested in how a certain object could be used," explains Giovanna, Achille's daughter, who, with her brother, Carlo, has set up the foundation Achille Castiglione. Here one can admire all the objects he designed, including the Luminator lamp that earned him his first *Compasso d'Oro* (one of the world's most famous industrial design awards) in 1955 – he won nine in total.

Also on display are many designs that never came to fruition at the time, like the Cubo armchair of 1957, then considered too modern but today produced by Meritalia. Or the now iconic arched floor lamp Arco de Flos (1962), created in an era when lamps were suspended from the ceiling – and one that could be moved around the room was inconceivable.

Prototypes are strewn around the studio, where scholars come to rummage through photos and drawings relating to Achille's prolific body of work; it includes 484 designs, 290 objects that were produced, and 190 architectural projects – not counting all the models for which there are no drawings because they were created on the spot, becoming the stuff of family legends. One, for instance, tells of how the invention of the 1972 Gibigiana lampshade saved the Castiglione marriage because it meant that Achille could read at night without disturbing his wife.

Some objects easily pass as contemporary, like the 1962 mayonnaise spoon with just the right curvature to clean the bottom of the jar, which is redistributed today by Alessi. Few people know that it was the Castiglionis who invented the *rompitratta* light switch in 1968, standard now on most European table lamps.

Address Piazza Castello 27, 20121 Milan, Tel +39 028053606, www.achillecastiglioni.it | **Getting there** Cadorna (M2 green line); Cairoli and Triennale (M1 red line); Carducci/Cadorna (bus 50, 58, 94); Buonaparte/Ricasoli (tram 1) | **Hours** By reservation only, Tue–Fri 10am, 11am and 12pm, Thu 6:30pm, 7:30pm and 8:30pm | **Tip** The old Palazzo del Verme was badly damaged during the war, but its magnificent Renaissance courtyard still remains. You have to know about it, since it is accessible only from the modern apartment block at Via Puccini 3.

91_ The Talisman at the Galleria

That bull's got lucky balls

Even though it is not in good taste to say it, if you really love Milan and want to come back, you must undergo the ceremony of the bull in the Galleria Vittorio Emanuele, and squash the bull's testicles in a series of rotations, while keeping your heel on the beast's family jewels. But what is even more embarrassing is the context in which this ritual takes place, since the animal is part of a mosaic on the floor beneath the central octagon's vault, in what is considered to be Milan's most elegant meet-up spot. Here, amid the monumental arches that link the Duomo to Piazza della Scala, framed by columns, stuccoes, and friezes, are some of the city's most historic cafés and shops.

The origin of this ritual is lost in time – it was likely pagan – but it is fun to imagine high-society women in the 19th-century strolling through the galleria and looking for the bull's "balls." Back then, the ritual was performed once a year, on December 31st, to bring good luck for the new year. Today, it is performed daily by hundreds of tourists, seriously compromising the animal's virility and forcing the city council to keep it under constant restoration.

The bull is depicted against a light blue background, at the center of the emblem of Turin, the first capital of the Kingdom of Italy. In 1865, the king of the House of Savoy himself laid the foundation stone of this monumental gallery. The tender was won by the architect Giuseppe Mengoni, who – as luck would have it – died on September 30th, 1887, on the eve of its opening. What a pity, just one more day and he could have rotated his foot on the bull and perhaps changed his destiny. But Mengoni was not a man of easy faith, as we can see from the work he left to the city: he made the daring choice to expose the iron supporting structure without sacrificing the overall elegance – something which showed a surprising modernity for the times.

Address Piazza Duomo, 20121 Milan | Getting there Duomo (M 1 red line, M 3 yellow line) | Tip In the Galleria is Camparino, the historic bar opened in 1915 by Davide Campari, where the Milanese go to have their aperitif. The sign was redesigned in 2012 by the artist Ugo Nespolo (www.camparino.it).

92__ Teatro 7 Lab

A kitchen on display

The kitchen is the star of the show at Via Thaon di Revel 7, especially in the evening, when the shop windows reflect light onto the street and you can glimpse inside to see a cooking class in action as would-be chefs hustle and bustle about. In the center of the kitchen is a high-tech stainless-steel counter behind which the apprentices skirt around pots and pans, engrossed in preparing a dinner that all the participants will eventually share.

The high point of the evening is the meal, during which the group makes observations and comments, but usually this doesn't happen before 11pm. There are many different themes to choose from, though the most popular courses are the ones dedicated to meat, fish, and rice, says Silvia Barbato, who runs the venue with her sister Maria.

Over the course of the evening you will learn how to select, cut, prepare, clean, marinate, and finally cook your meal, which usually includes three to four recipes. Roberto Cuculo, despite his young age, is already an award-winning personal chef, and it's his task to coordinate the clumsy and disorganized novices, until the suspense is over and it is time to see whether the final result will be met by cheers or groans. Even food-loving kids can become mini chefs.

To passersby, the convivial group might well seem like a theatrical troupe rehearsing a play with a wall of ovens as its backdrop. TV food celebrities occasionally drop by to film a cooking show, but that doesn't take away from the kitchen's simple, homey atmosphere – its electric appliances and tableware are the same as those you would find in any private kitchen.

Whether you decide to go for a class on appetizers, the latest sushi trends, or traditional *agnolotti*, be prepared to get your hands dirty. If you're looking for a way to spend an unusual evening with your friends, this is the place for you.

Address Via Giovanni Thaon di Revel 7, 20159 Milan, Tel +39 0289073719, www.teatro7.com | **Getting there** Zara (M 3 yellow line); Isola (M 5 lilac line); Lambertenghi (tram 7) | **Hours** Check the website | **Tip** The Deus Cafe is a bar that originated in Australia from the combination of three passions: motorcycles, bikes, and surfing. It can be found in the courtyard of Via Thaon di Revel 3 (Mon–Sun 9:30am–1am, www.deuscustoms.com).

93 __ Torre Branca
The Fernet terrace

From a distance it looks like a very high trellis soaring above the trees in Sempione Park. The tower – 350 feet high, quite a feat when it was constructed in 1933 – was originally called Torre Littoria, from the Latin *fascio littorio*, a bundle of wood that the *lictors* (members of an ancient Roman class of magisterial attendants), used as weapons. It became a Fascist symbol and is actually at the origin of the term *fascism*.

Today, the tower is known as Torre Branca. It was built at a time when Italy was recovering from World War I and Milan was experiencing rapid industrial growth. The architects Cesare Chiodi and Giò Ponti designed a pyramid-like structure, made entirely of steel tubes that would defy the sky in lightness and strength. The whole structure is held together by flanges and bolts; a precursor of future skyscrapers – and what we would call today "an exercise in style." The tower is 20 feet wide at the base and 15 feet wide at the top. It took only 68 days to build, but in terms of design it was way ahead of its time, and it remains one of the city's highest structures.

Torre Branca was commissioned for the fifth edition of the Triennale of Milan exhibition – "to rise high," as Giò Ponti put it – but was closed in 1972 as the structure was deemed unsafe. It remained so until 2002, when the Branca family, known for its famous Fernet liquor, decided to finance its restoration and return this symbol of industrial archaeology to the city.

Today everyone can pay homage to such an audacious project by drinking a glass of Fernet on the top floor terrace. In less than a minute, a state-of-the-art elevator takes you to the observation platform, from where you can admire the spectacular panorama of the city. Only five people at a time are allowed on the platform, on which the first RAI (the Italian state radio/TV company) antenna was installed in 1939.

Address Parco Sempione, Viale Luigi Camoens, 20121 Milan, Tel +39 023314120 |
Getting there Cadorna Triennale (M 2 green line) | Hours Summer: Tues, Thu and Fri
3–7pm and 8:30pm–midnight, Wed, Sat and Sun, open also in the morning. Winter:
Sept 15–May 15; Wed 10:30am–12:30pm and 4–6:30pm, Sat 10:30am–1pm,
3–6:30pm and 8:30pm–midnight, Sun 10:30am–7pm. Closed in bad weather | Tip
At Via Resegone 2 is the museum that tells the history of the Branca family and brand.
The family's eagle emblem hangs over the factory's entrance; you can visit some of the
original rooms, among them the distillery and the herb laboratory (www.branca.it,
Tel +39 028513970).

94__ Toti

A submarine in the heart of the city

Like some gigantic marine monster, it skirted just below the water's surface with its 300 tons of steel and 140-foot-long body. It was the first of a new generation of spy submarines that the Italian navy unveiled in the spring of 1967, at the height of the Cold War. When this giant steel whale was finally put out to dry after 30 years of honorable service, the navy decided to donate it to the city of Milan. And that's when the real challenges began.

The story of the *Enrico Toti* S 506 submarine soon made headlines, as heaps of technicians, engineers, and security personnel were called in to organize its colossal transport: a five-year journey from Sicily to the Po Valley that was meticulously documented in video and photos. The voyage began in 2000 with its submersion at the military port of Augusta.

After restoration work, the sub was towed to Taranto, and then, after 85 hours of navigation, it entered the delta of the river Po, at Chioggia. People lined the banks of the canal to see "Toti," as it was affectionately called, being towed by two tugboats. On May 6 it triumphantly arrived at Cremona, where it was moored. At that point the Polytechnic University of Milan began to study the last leg of the journey, which had to be done by land since the old canals of the Navigli, for which da Vinci had perfected a system of locks, were not designed to transport vessels of this size. First of all, the lead ballast was removed, which shaved 20 tons off the submarine's weight. Then a custom-designed 240-wheel vehicle was built – 200 feet long, 15 feet wide, and more than 20 feet high. In Milan, signposts, sidewalks, traffic lights, and power lines had to be removed to make way for the convoy.

Toti finally arrived in town on the night of August 13, 2005. Today you can admire the vessel in all its glory at the national science museum, and wonder how the heck it ever got there.

Address Museo Nazionale della Scienza Leonardo da Vinci, Via San Vittore 21, 20123 Milan, Tel +39 02485551, www.museoscienza.org / toti | **Getting there** Sant'Ambrogio (M 2 green line); San Vittore (bus 50); Carducci (bus 94) | **Hours** Tue – Fri 10am – 6pm, Sat – Sun 10am – 7pm | **Tip** At Via Matteo Bandello 14 you can visit the gallery run by Rossana Orlandi, who exhibits very particular interior design objects (www.rossanaorlandi.com).

95_ Thieves in the Window

*A gallery of stained glass in the Veneranda Fabbrica
del Duomo*

More often than not, the stained-glass windows in cathedrals are out of sight of the human eye. This is because their main purpose was a practical, not an aesthetic, one: to filter light inside the nave.

It is thus sadly the fate of many glassmakers to see their work go unappreciated, and their place in history unacknowledged. At least until now, that is: a long overdue homage to their artistry and expertise has finally arrived in the form of an evocative exhibition hosted in the museum of the Duomo's Veneranda Fabbrica (Venerable Factory).

To reach the windows you first have to pass through a maze of sculptures, zoomorphic faces – openmouthed monsters and dragons that served as rain gutters, and inlaid spires in every shape and dimension. The room's design is slick and modern, its dim lighting aimed at bringing to life the vivid colors of the 32 backlit windows, all designed between the 12th and 16th centuries.

In one window you will find two thieves hanging on the cross: the good one looking up, as if confiding in divine hope; the bad one looking down, grimacing, with a snake (the devil) breathing down his neck. The cerulean sky is filled with the arabesques of menacing clouds. Everything is visible down to the tiniest detail: the muscles on the chest, the golden curls of the beard, the forced bending of the legs, the compression of the pelvis due to the uncomfortable position.

The window, which dates back to the 16th century, is the work of Nordic masters, descendants of a long tradition of workers in the Gothic cathedrals. Originally, it was located in the large opening of the apse dedicated to the New Testament, next to the crucifixion of Christ. Then, in the 19th century, during some restoration work, the thieves were taken down. Today we can finally admire the exquisite craftsmanship of glassmaker Corrado de'Mochis in all its glory.

Address Museo del Duomo, Piazza Duomo 12, 20122 Milan, Tel +39 02860358, www.museo.duomomilano.it | Getting there Duomo (M1 red line and M3 yellow line) | Hours Tue–Sun 10am–6pm (last entrance 4:45pm) | Tip At Via delle Ore 3, next door to the Arcivescovado, is the Ambrosianeum, a curious decagonal building from the 16th century known for its inner circle room supported by columns, which today houses the Ambrosianeum Foundation (www.ambrosianeum.org).

96__ Triennale

Happy Hour surrounded by sculptures

Pietra Sonora (Musical Stone), La Fontana dei Bagni Misteriosi (The Fountain of Mysterious Baths), Luna Caduta in Basso (Fallen Moon), Continuità (Continuity): these are just some of the names of the sculptures exhibited outside in the gardens of the Triennale. There are thirteen open-air works in total, including pieces by artists Giorgio de Chirico (1973), Ettore Sottsass (2005), Pinuccio Sciola (2010), and even architect Andreas Wenning (for the Baumraun studio), famous for his tree houses.

You can reach this corner of the Sempione Park from the Triennale building, opened in 1933 under the direction of Giò Ponte and Mario Sironi. The exhibition area is in the middle of a lawn that would make the British proud.

On a sunny day you'll be tempted to sit on the three armchairs by the artist Gaetano Pesce (2005): the "ladies" (as they are nicknamed) sport sinuous, rounded, and prosperous bodies like those of Neolithic Venuses. If only they weren't made of bronze, you could imagine sinking into their softness. Oh well, c'est la vie: best to make do with the slimline chairs of the open-air cafe, which, in any case, are not your run-of-the-mill seats, but designer chairs set out on a rotating basis from a collection of about 100. It is like a museum within the museum.

The Triennale is an open space – in every sense of the word, with an important permanent collection of fashion and design objects that are being curated and displayed constantly. Its 130,000 square feet host temporary exhibitions (with an entrance fee), theater performances, and shows that run the gamut of all fields of creativity, including digital technology. After all, the new Palazzo dell'Arte, designed by Giovanni Muzio for the fifth Triennale (when the Torre Branca was first opened to the public), was intended to promote unity in the arts, which it continues to do to this day.

Address Viale Emilio Alemagna, 6, 20121 Milan, Tel +39 02724341,
www.triennale.it | Getting there Cadorna (M 2 green line); Triennale (bus 61) | Hours
Tue–Sun 10:30am–8:30pm, Thu open till 11pm | Tip In Piazza Cadorna you can view
Ago, Filo e Nodo (*Needle, Thread, and Knot*), a public artwork by Claes Oldenburg and
Coosje van Bruggen. The knot is a few meters from the needle but joined to it
metaphorically by the metro. The work was commissioned for the opening of the new
railway station (Cadorna) in 2000, but the Milanese are not particularly fond of it.

97__ The Turtle Lake

The DIY aquarium in Forlanini Park

Yes, Forlanini Park has a small lake. But you have to know where to find it (most Milanese do) since it is somewhat out of the way and not that easy to stumble upon. But the park does have a convenient side entrance that allows you to reach the lake by car.

This is where families come, after presumably long and emotional debates, to release their overgrown pet turtles into the wild. "It's eaten all the plants." "It's gotten too big for the aquarium." "It will be so much happier in the beautiful lake with all its 'friends.'" These are some of the classic excuses that parents use to try to convince their reluctant children to set their beloved charges free.

Although it is technically prohibited to deposit pet turtles in the park, it has nonetheless become a Milanese custom over the years. At first the size of a fist, over time these delightful reptiles become veritable aquatic monsters that can no longer be contained in home aquariums. And you can't exactly wait for them to die, given that a turtle of the *Trachemys* species, which most pet turtles are, can live up to 40 years.

In any case, they *do* seem to enjoy it here in the park. The problem is that due to the numerous contributions to the lake, the turtles have become invasive and have started to damage the existing eco-system. If you walk around the perimeter of the lake you can see dozens of them, especially on a warm day, when they climb above the few rocks on the water's edge to catch some rays. They may well appreciate a few extra sunbeds. Originating in the swamps of the United States, the turtles have grown accustomed to humans, although they still like to maintain a safe distance of at least 30 feet.

The steep lawn offers an excellent vantage point from which to study the crowded colony's behavior. The kids love it, but who's to say that a more sinister amphibian hasn't been released into the waters?

Address Viale Enrico Forlanini (toward the center) and Strada Rivoltana-Via Salesina, 20134 Milan | Getting there Forlanini (bus 73); Centro Saini (bus 38) | Tip In 2001, at Linate Airport, due to fog, a plane crashed into a Cessna that had found itself on the wrong runway, causing the death of 118 passengers. To commemorate this tragic event, 118 trees have been planted in an area of Forlanini Park called Bosco dei Faggi (Beech Tree Wood).

98_ The Twin Churches
Communication strategies of a betrayed duchess

The Italian saying, *due cuori una chiesa* ("two hearts one church") is certainly true of Santa Maria Incoronata. The original building had only one principal entry façade – the one seen on the left when you observe the church from the square. The other entry façade, almost identical to the original one, came later.

The Augustinian convent at the back of the church is dedicated to Santa Maria di Garegnano (located where the chapels II and III are today) and was added at the beginning of the 15th century. Subsequently, the Lombard Congregation of the Order of Saint Augustine set out to enlarge the convent. The renovation ended in 1451, the year Francesco Sforza became Duke of Milan. To celebrate this event the monks renamed the church Incoronata ("enthroned").

The rest we owe to Francesco Sforza's wife, Bianca Maria Visconti. Angered and tired of listening to the constant rumors about her husband's affairs, she had the inspired idea to have an additional entry façade and corresponding nave built in 1460 to mirror the existing one, as a very public testament to the couple's love and fidelity. As you walk into the church you can see the two adjoining naves that together constitute one single church.

Bianca Maria Visconti was the illegitimate yet beloved daughter of Filippo Maria Visconti, who was Duke of Milan before Francesco Sforza. She was a woman known to possess an extraordinary amount of political know-how. The history books describe her as cultured, intelligent, and extremely imaginative – all traits that were clearly exemplified in this cunning scheme.

It must have been a combination of political necessity and personal ingenuity that led her to come up with such an original solution: twinned façades that would always remind the city of the sacred union that bound together her family until the death of the adulterous duke, with whom she had eight children.

Address Corso Garibaldi 116, 20121 Milan | Getting there Moscova (M2 green line) |
Hours Mon–Sun 8:30am–7pm | Tip Behind the church is the 15th-century cloister
and the convent's Biblioteca Umanistica (humanistic library), which contained many
priceless volumes (now at the Biblioteca Ambrosiana). Completely frescoed, it is used
for exhibitions and concerts.

99__ Ulrico Hoepli Planetarium
Where the stars are always out

From the outside it looks like any old neoclassical temple with the *pronaos* supported by four Doric columns. But inside, this long-loved planetarium transforms into a starlit city.

A true piece of scientific archaeology, nowadays it comes across as a little bit derelict, but in its day it was at the cutting edge of technological experimentation. The Swiss philanthropist Ulrico Hoepli donated it to the city on July 10th, 1929, with these words: "To the generous city of Milan, my adopted home, I donate, with grateful heart, this Planetarium." The project was commissioned to architect Piero Portaluppi, a real and proper "starchitect" of the times, and took almost a year to be completed.

The building was inaugurated by Mussolini on May 20th, 1930, amid great enthusiasm and excitement, especially among Milanese astrophysicists, who were already at the forefront in their field. Hoepli even founded a publishing house (to disseminate the studies conducted at the Brera observatory) and a wonderful bookstore, just behind the Duomo, which still exists today.

The Brera Institute could also count on an annex in Brianza (north of Milan), where the sky could be studied far from the city's light pollution. The idea of building a planetarium in the gardens of Porta Venezia aroused such curiosity that in 1937, a 35mm German-made Zeiss projector was installed to screen the first scientific films ever made.

Thanks to this new and sophisticated piece of equipment, the great cupola was transformed into a gigantic celestial dome onto which the movement of the stars and planets was projected. It is heartwarming to see the round wooden seats, which have welcomed thousands of spectators over the years to experience the first documentaries about the secrets of the universe. Sixty-five feet wide, this is the largest celestial dome in Italy – a real "window into the infinite."

Address Corso Venezia 57 (next door to the Natural History Museum), 20121 Milan, Tel +39 0288463340 | **Getting there** Palestro (M 1 red line); Oberdan (tram 9) | **Hours** Mon–Fri 9am–1pm (and for conferences) | **Tip** The Brera astronomical observatory, founded in 1762, is now a museum. You can visit the cupola and the collection of historical instruments, which includes two 17th-century globes – one celestial and the other terrestrial (Via Brera 28, Mon–Fri 8:30am–4:30pm, guided tours at 1pm on Wednesdays, www.brera.mi.astro.it)

100_ Urbicus, the Gladiator

All that remains of the Roman amphitheater

Okay, so it's not in great shape – with its spray-painted outer walls, it looks more like a run-down school than an archaeological park. However, once you enter the former convent on Via de Amicis, a fascinating surprise awaits you: the actual ruins of a Roman amphitheater, where gladiatorial games and lion fights took place.

Begin at the Antiquarium Alda Levi, dedicated to the Jewish archaeologist who was persecuted under Fascism. The collection of artifacts on display – which includes clasps, terra-cotta statues, vases, amphorae, jewels, and other objects in bronze and bone – was unearthed during the excavation of the nearby arena, which no longer exists. It covered a vast area between the Conca del Naviglio and Corso di Porta Ticinese. Various display cabinets explain the history of the place.

Each object illuminates an aspect of daily life at the time of *Mediolanum*: how a pharmacy was organized, how a house was built, and what it meant to pursue a career as a gladiator. The latter is revealed in the precious funeral stele dedicated to Urbicus (3rd century AD), a formidable fighter who certainly didn't lack courage, seeing as he was a *secutor* – that is, a "follower," or "chaser." The role of the *secutor* in the fierce games that took place in the arena – and which ended in the death of the loser – was to incite the competitors and to enliven the spectacle.

Urbicus is depicted wearing a short tunic and carrying a sword; his left arm holds a curved shield and on his right leg is a shin pad. He was only 22 years old when he died, but he already had thirteen victories under his belt. He left behind two daughters, a 5-month-old and a 7-year-old, and his wife, Laurica, who dedicated this minutely written epigraph to him: "I warn you, kill the opponent whom you defeat, whoever he may be. His fans will keep his memory alive." Honor indeed to the glory of Urbicus.

Address Antiquarium / Anfiteatro Alda Levi, Via Edmondo de Amicis 17, 20123, Tel +39 0289400555 | **Getting there** Colonne San Lorenzo (bus 94); Piazza Resistenza Partigiana (tram 2, 14) | **Hours** Antiquarium: Tue – Sat 9:30am – 2pm. Amphitheater: Tue – Fri 9am – 4:30pm (winter), 9am – 6pm (summer), Sat 9am – 2pm | **Tip** In the Basilica di Sant'Eustorgio, you can visit the paleo-Christian necropolis dating back to the 3rd and 4th centuries AD, with its many funeral epigraphs.

101_ The Vertical Forest

"Growing up" in the city

In a city with relatively few green areas, the Studio Boeri had a brilliant idea: Why not build a "vertical forest"? The result is a pair of high-rises – 18 and 26 stories respectively – with giant cantilevered, staggered balconies that accommodate a number of large plants and trees.

The towers' "ecosystem" will encompass as many as 900 species with 5,000 varieties of shrubs and 15,000 types of perennials, say the biologists and botanists who were charged with selecting the flora best suited for the different levels of sun exposure. These include almond trees, cherry trees, ash trees, alder trees, vines, and – of course – a plethora of different flowers.

One may wonder: what is expected of the residents? Replacing a dead oak or olive tree is one thing, but shelling out for a new "Regina Claudia" plum tree is another matter altogether. No need to worry: a team of gardeners and biologists will always be on hand to offer support. The "vertical towers" are more than just buildings – they are a collective project of like-minded people. This also requires following rather strict botanical guidelines (so no herbs and spices on the balcony, I'm afraid). On the upside, the buildings are equipped with a centralized irrigation system, so residents don't have to worry about watering. They can only pray bugs won't take up residence inside their apartments, since parasite control is strictly organic: insects vs. insects (1,200 ladybugs have already been unleashed to fight aphids). But a whole bunch of other animals also have been enlisted in the "war on pests": butterflies, bats, etc., depending on the season.

Like it or not, this is the next stage in the evolution of urban green: solutions that are both pleasing to the eye and the lungs (more plants mean more oxygen and cleaner air). "Only time will tell," say the developers of the project, which is the first of its kind.

Address Via Gaetano de Castillia, 20124 Milan | Getting there Gioia and Garibaldi (M2 green line); Garibaldi (tram 33; bus 37) | Tip At number 28 on the same street, in a building dating back to the early 20th century, are the offices of the Riccardo Catella Foundation. Here also is one of the most exclusive restaurants in town, the Ratanà (Tel +39 0287128855, www.ratana.it).

102 __ Via Bagnera

The street of the serial killer

Via Bagnera in the Carrobbio district has a sinister reputation – and it's completely deserved. Snubbed by the surrounding buildings, all of which have their backs turned to it, it is so narrow you can only access it on foot, and if you spread your arms you can actually touch the walls on both sides. Not even the probing eye of Google's "street view" can penetrate it.

Even though it is located just behind the well-to-do Via Torino, this lane is pretty beat up. Nonetheless, a conscientious traffic warden has painted a zebra crossing at the exit onto Via Santa Maria. There are only three white stripes – there wasn't room for more.

The street's atmosphere is both fascinating and disturbing; it feels as if at any moment a mugger might jump out at you. It's a no man's land right in the heart of the city, well known to graffiti artists as well as lovers of true crime, due to its bloody past.

No reason to be afraid now, though – the events that contributed to Via Bagnera's dark history happened more than 150 years ago, when a serial killer prowled the area for 10 years, before finally being apprehended. The victims – a shopkeeper, a businessman, a worker, and a wealthy lady – were robbed of their money and then cut into pieces. Their bodies were found in the cellar of one of buildings on Via Bagnera.

The "monster," once captured, appeared on the surface to be an average, ordinary individual, as is so often the case. He was a builder, a doorman, and finally, a serial killer who would pick his victims carefully, gaining their trust and then inviting them into his macabre cellar.

When he was hanged, Milan breathed a sigh of relief. The year was 1861, and this was the last capital punishment decreed by the city's tribunal. But the sinister air of Via Bagnera is still perceptible today – especially at sunset, at least according to the ghost busters.

Address Via Bagnera, 20123 Milan | **Getting there** Duomo (M 1 red line, M 3 yellow line); Torino (tram 2, 14) | **Tip** The streets between Sant'Ambrogio and Via San Maurilio, known as "the five-street district," have a totally different feel from Via Bagnera: charming, trendy, chic, and exclusive. The designer Uberta Zambeletti's Wait and See shop, at Via Santa Marta 14, is more than just a shop: it is a veritable art gallery displaying the latest trends in cutting-edge fashion.

103_ Via Paolo Sarpi

Milan's very own Chinatown

It all started with a small Chinese restaurant nestled between a stationery shop and an old grocery store. A Chinese restaurant like so many others: orange lanterns, egg rolls, dumplings, and all the rest. Then another one popped up, and another, and slowly but surely, the Chinese community ended up taking over one of Milan's most authentic streets.

It was once a typical middle-class neighborhood, where the shopkeepers, doormen, and newsagents knew all the residents by name. But there is no point in dwelling on the past: these days on Via Sarpi the Italian and Chinese communities coexist quite nicely, even though communication between them is not always fluid (to make things easier for everyone, the shop windows have bilingual signs). The street is now a pedestrian-friendly zone, and a residents' association is responsible for maintaining the flowerbeds, the pendulum clocks, and the brightly colored advertisements in yellow and dragon red.

The shops sell almost everything you can think of: from mobile phones to computer components (at the Via Rosmini end), from Chinese noodles to freeze-dried food, from wigs to Manga paper tissues. The logic is unfathomable but it seems to work from a commercial standpoint.

Halfway down the street, in the big gold-lettered Oriental Mall, two young girls with straight, long black hair hurriedly eat their takeaway lunch on the shop's counter among bras, T-shirts, necklaces, makeup, baby bibs, cushions, and pink envelopes. Next door is the food market Hu Foods. The local Italian housewives are still somewhat reluctant to buy their groceries here, even though the fresh produce comes from the city's main fruit and vegetable market, as it does in any other grocery store. They find the old hardware store or the Melegari hat shop at number 19 – here since 1914 and an authentic Milanese designer – much more reassuring.

Address Via Paolo Sarpi, 20154 Milan | **Getting there** Moscova (M 2 green line); Canonica / Sarpi (bus 43, 57); Gramsci (bus 37); Bramante / Sarpi (tram 12, 14) | **Tip** On Via Canonica (at the corner of Via Moscati) there is a very good Sicilian homemade ice-cream shop, Vasavasa. Its fresh ingredients are chosen with great care, resulting in truly excellent fruit sorbets (Mon–Sun 12pm–midnight, www.vasavasa-it).

104_ Vicolo dei Lavandai
When men did the washing

Let's bust the myth that in the days before running water and washing machines, doing the wash by the riverbank was a task for women alone. In the 19th century, this was not always the case. Not in Milan, at least, where laundry was actually considered a man's job. Families that could afford it, in fact, would bring their dirty clothes and bedding to the Confraternita dei Lavandai (Fraternity of Washmen), an organization dating back to the 18th century made up entirely of men.

The fraternity also had its own patron saint: none other than Saint Anthony of Padua, to whom one of the altars in the church of Santa Maria delle Grazie, on the Alzaia Naviglio Grande, is dedicated. The church is not far from the street that still bears the name Vicolo dei Lavandai (Washmen's Alley).

This corner of the Naviglio, near Porta Ticinese, preserves a glimpse of the old days. Various courtyards and warehouses look out onto this closed-in *piazzetta* covered with hard-packed earth and bordered with plants, where the merchants used to unload their boats.

On the other side flows *el fosset*, a little stream that draws its water from the Naviglio. The washing basins are still here, positioned side by side under a wooden roof. In later years, the place became more of a women's domain: the older shopkeepers still remember how they would arrive with their buckets, kneel down, and use the stone blocks as washboards. This lasted up until the late 1950s (a photo dated 1957 shows the author Georges Simenon with the washwomen in the background).

Even back then, poets and writers were attracted to the spot's evocative and nostalgic atmosphere. The old grocery store that sold floor brushes, soap, and bleach is now a quaint restaurant that has kept the original fittings and ceiling. In one of the courtyards you can also see one of the first spin dryers.

Address Alzaia Naviglio Grande, Vicolo dei Lavandai, 20144 Milan | Getting there
Porta Genova (M 2 green line); Cantore / Porta Genova (tram 14, 19 and bus 47, 74);
Gorizia (tram 9) | Tip You can get to Vicolo dei Lavandai from Via Vigevano 9.
A series of beautiful earth-covered courtyards reveals the charm of the old houses of
the Naviglio; just open the gate at the end and you are there.

105 __ Villa Invernizzi

A courtyard of flamingos

It's hard to describe how surprising it is to come upon a group of flamingos in the center of Milan – just a stone's throw from Corso Venezia – among the large magnolia trees on the other side of the iron railings that surround the Invernizzi Villa. This is the house of the founder of the famous Mio soft cheese that generations of Italian kids have grown up eating.

There they stand, on one leg, with their necks bent and their beaks submerged in their pink feathers (they're picking out the fleas, if you're wondering), as if it was the most comfortable position in the world.

Though truly an unexpected encounter, it befits a city as unpredictable as Milan, which often keeps its secrets hidden away in living rooms and private courtyards. This one, at least, is partly open to the public, allowing you to admire the flamingos from the street. A small crowd of intrigued passersby, usually families with small children, gathers every day in front of the gates of the villa. Even more come now that the park's old zoo is closed.

The colony of flamingos seems totally at home here, entrusted to the loving care of the custodian who every day prepares tasty delicacies of shellfish for the birds. A correct diet is fundamental to preserving their beautiful blushing plumage. A small lake keeps the flock cool in summer. They have adapted well and show no signs of wanting to leave – in fact, they have actually started to reproduce at such a rate that a team of vets periodically has to move some birds to another location. The flamingos you see today have all been born in captivity, but their ancestors came from South America and Africa.

The flamingo courtyard is an exotic oasis right in the heart of Milan that exists thanks to the will and testament of Sir Invernizzi (he was knighted in 1966), and is today considered part and parcel of the city's heritage.

Address Via Cappuccini 3, 20122 Milan | Getting there Palestro (M1 red line)
Monforte/Donizetti (bus 54, 61) | Tip At the corner of Via Vivaio and Via Cappuccini
is the Berri-Meregalli house, designed by the architect Giulio Ulisse Arata at the
beginning of the 20th century. It is richly decorated with extraordinary mosaics and
polychrome figures that represent the final phase of the Art Nouveau period.

106__ Villa Necchi Campiglio

Ahead of its time

The 1930s swimming pool in the villa's garden was the first one ever constructed in the city. It was part of a residence that would have been perfectly at home in the countryside. But that wouldn't have given the Necchi Campiglio family what it wanted: a country house right in the heart of Milan's historical center, with all the comforts that modern life could offer. Half an acre of land and no financial limitations – it was every architect's dream!

In 1932, the lucky assignment was given to the architect of the moment, the innovative Piero Portaluppi. The credit for the project's rationalist style, crafty technological solutions, avant-garde design, and intelligent use of new materials – like the beautiful door in copper, zinc, and silver alloy to hide the garden in winter – goes entirely to Portaluppi.

The industrialist Angelo Campiglio lived here with his wife, Gigina Necchi (of the famous sewing machine brand), and her sister Nedda. You can almost picture them standing at the elegant front door to welcome their many illustrious friends.

The living room is a veritable museum, its walls adorned with rare paintings by Giorgio Morandi, as well as some fine originals by the likes of Sironi, Arturo Martini, and de Chirico.

Nothing has been changed in the house since Gigina's death in 2001 – which might be why it still feels lived in. The carpet in the smoking room has been burned in spots by the late-night cigarettes savored in front of the fireplace – all that is missing are the ashtrays full of butts.

Modernity was a good thing, but the Necchi Campiglios were also careful not to offend the sensibilities of their blue-blood friends, such as the princes and princesses of the Savoia family. Hence the 18th-century-style salon and luxury bedrooms on the first floor were designed to make even the most traditional-minded guests feel at home.

Address Via Mozart 14, 20122 Milan, Tel +39 0276340121, www.fondoambiente.it |
Getting there Palestro (M 1 red line), Montenapoleone (M 3 yellow line); San
Damiano/Monforte (bus 54, 61, 94) | Hours Wed–Sun 10am–6pm (managed by the
FAI, Fondo Ambiente Italiano, booking is advisable) | Tip At Via Mozart 21 is the
Berri-Meregalli house, designed in 1910 by Giulio Ulisse Arata (1881–1962). The
architect was compared to Gaudì for his eclecticism. The figures on the façade are by
Rimoldi and the wrought-iron work is by the famous metal craftsman Mazzuccotelli.

107__ Villa Simonetta

The echo of young love

The delightful Villa Simonetta was always known for its famous echo, which would befit a music academy. In 1726, the Italian writer Marc'Antonio del Re praised it in his book on the most beautiful villas of Milan: "It reverberates the same voice up to thirty and more times," he wrote, though he noted that the effect could only be obtained "from a window on the third floor at the center of the western side, facing the inner courtyard." Such specificity lends credibility to his assertion.

Built at the end of the 15th century as the country home of Chancellor Ludovico il Moro, in 1547 the villa was transformed by the Gonzaga family into a sumptuous state residence before passing into the hands of the Simonetta family. Stendhal, who loved Italy well, insisted on sojourning at the villa, and recounts in his memories that a shot fired accidently from his pistol echoed 50 times. This has given rise to countless legends over the years; allegedly, lovers would lean out of the window to listen to their passion-filled whispers over and over again. Such tales were fueled by the fact that the local blue-blooded youth would gather at the villa – probably chosen for its convenient location far from prying eyes – for their bohemian parties, earning it, in the early 19th century, the moniker of *villa dei balabiott* ("villa of naked dancers" in Lombard dialect). The legend of Clelia Simonetta, the beautiful widow who would seduce and then murder her lovers, dates back to this period.

Some believe that the lady's ghostly figure still roams the galleries of this magnificent cloister, though the echo of the young lovers was probably blasted away by bombs that hit the villa during World War II, ruining forever its magical sound effect.

Today those words of love are replaced by the music of the Civica Scuola di Musica Claudio Abbado, and by the concerts held in the park during the summer.

Address Via Stilicone 36, 20154 Milan, Tel +39 02971524, www.fondazionemilano.eu/musica | **Getting there** Garibaldi and Lanza (M2 green line); Govone/Eugenio (bus 78); Cenisio/Messina (tram 12, 14) | **Hours** Anytime, by booking in advance; or during one of the many concerts held here (see website) | **Tip** The Academy also has a frescoed chapel that hosts a multimedia library containing 8,000 accessible works of sheet music (Tel +39 0297152429, times: Mon–Fri 10am–12:30pm/2:30–5pm) and manages the Auditorium Lattuada at Corso Porta Vigentina 15/a (Tel +39 02 58314433).

108_ The Wall of Dolls

To end violence against women

It is not the window of a toy shop, although you'd be forgiven for wanting to take one of those beautiful dolls home with you. The multicolored figures are attached to the mesh wall of the Casa dei Diritti in Porta Ticinese, and every day a new one is added. You may wonder then, why are they there?

The *Wall of Dolls* is an art installation aimed at raising awareness about violence against women, conceived by the versatile artist Jo Squillo, who has enlisted the support of several associations and celebrities, as well as the participation of at least 50 fashion houses. After all, how many clothing designers started out as children who made clothes for their dolls? It began in the summer of 2014 on the opening day of men's fashion week in Milan. And since the issue is still widespread, the silent voices of the dolls have become a permanent scream. The oldest dolls are a little jaded – the fabric of their dresses have faded in the sun and their lips are pale – but new ones are arriving all the time, joyous, puffy-cheeked, curly-haired, and long-legged. Don't be misled by their smiles, though; they are very, very angry.

Children are particularly intrigued by the dolls and always insist on looking at them closely. "What does the wall mean?" they ask their parents. The answer is: be aware. Some of the phrases hanging on the wall really bring the message home: "If you read the news about crime you realize that the enemy is closer than you think … in the family!"

The dolls are nameless, just like the female victims of domestic violence who they represent – one in three in Europe, according to the statistics. And there are all kinds of dolls: sweet, modern, disheveled, sexy, young, old, and made of plastic or cloth – from the timeless Barbie to the South-American *mamita* in her poncho. Anyone is free to add his or her own doll to the wall – a multicultural message in a female-friendly city.

Address Via Edmondo De Amicis 2, 20123 Milan | Getting there Ticinese
(bus 94, 163); Correnti (tram 2, 14) | Tip At Via Arena 7 is the Sorelle Riva plant
nursery, a small jungle of potted plants, azaleas, and jasmines, run by two ladies with a
green thumb. The place has become the benchmark for locals wanting to revamp their
terraces. They also organize workshops for children and aperitifs for adults in a lovely
botanical setting (Mon–Sat 8:30am–12:30pm and 2:30–6:30pm).

109__ The Wanton Woman
Federico Barbarossa's wife

As you stroll through the museum in the Sforza Castle, you may stumble upon a curious marble tablet nestled among the solemn soldiers on horseback, the somber statues, and the various Virgin Marys. It was once in full view on the façade of the Porta Tosa Arch, one of the gateways into the city, renamed Porta Vittoria (Victory Gate) after the Unification of Italy.

Today it is hidden away in a small, dark corner of room VI, which is dedicated to the history of medieval Milan. It is easy to see why it suffered such a fate, even though few people actually notice it due to the poor lighting: it depicts a woman combing her pubic hair, just like that.

In the 12th century it was a habit for prostitutes to perform this as part of their hygiene, to remove lice. What is curious is that the woman depicted on the tablet is wearing a long tunic and has a crown keeping her hair up, just as if she were a princess framed within a classical niche. These regal attributes, despite the simplicity of the composition, were fodder for the gossipers, who decided that it was a portrait of the wife of Federico Barbarossa, the loathed emperor who had literally razed Milan to the ground in 1162.

Tradition would have it that in discrediting him, one had to mock his wife Leobissa as well. This is perhaps why the lewd portrait of the empress – then given the name Tosa, which in Milanese dialect means "young girl" – was hung on the gate of the city. Whether she was the wife of Barbarossa or not, it was considered distasteful by the ultra-chaste Carlo Borromeo, who in 1566 became archbishop of Milan and swiftly removed the bas-relief that had been the object of such vulgar ridicule.

Today it is thought that the tablet represents a votive image of Celtic origin soliciting good luck. In the meantime "Queen Leobissa" is safe within the walls of the castle.

Address Castello Sforzesco, Piazza Castello, 20121 Milan, Tel +39 0288463700, www.milanocastello.it | **Getting there** Cairoli (M1 red line); Cadorna (M2 green line); Cairoli (tram 1; bus 50, 61) | **Hours** Tue–Sun 9am–5pm | **Tip** Speaking of unconventional female sculptures, it is worth taking a look at the *Pietà Rondanini* by Michelangelo in the former Ospedale Spagnolo, currently under renovation, located inside the castle's courtyard.

110__ The Workshops of La Scala

Behind the scenes of the famous theater

Just like the Duomo, La Scala has its own "Venerable Factory": a 200,000-square-foot pavilion located in the former Ansaldo di Porta Genova industrial area. Here, 150 people – technicians, mechanics, carpenters, seamstresses, and costume designers – are always at work. It takes from three to four months – and a life-size replica of the Piermarini stage in La Scala – to prepare for an opera like *Fidelio* or *Aida*.

This factory contributes to the prestige of La Scala, one of the few theaters in the world that has the means to create an entire stage production on its own, from start to finish, all the way from the early sketches to opening night. When the lights finally go down and the red velvet curtains open, everything you see is "made in La Scala."

Behind the scenes of this massive structure, which would fit right in at a Hollywood studio, are the workshops where the colorful backdrops and polystyrene sculptures are made. Particularly impressive are the enormous bridge cranes in the mechanics' workshop, used to assemble the scenery, and the costume department's corridors, littered with outfits ready to be sent to the theater, among which you might recognize those of Violetta from *La Traviata* or Mimì from *La Bohème*.

Under the direction of the costume designers, the seamstresses cut, sew, dye, crease, and age the material. Of course, if they are beginning a job, all you may see are mannequins wearing paper patterns. The end result must be perfect: nowadays, with TV, every little detail can be seen. There are 1,500 wardrobes in total, each containing 60 to 70 costumes, the oldest ones dating back to the 1920s. There is always a selection of historic costumes on display, corresponding to the shows onstage at the time. Some have even been worn by Pavarotti, Nureyev, or Callas.

Address Laboratori Ansaldo-La Scala, Via Bergognone 34 (at Via Tortona), 20144 Milan, www.teatrolascala.org | **Getting there** Porta Genova (M2 green line; bus 47, 74, 170, 325); Bergognone (bus 68) | **Hours** Tues and Thu, advance booking required (Associazione Civita, Tel +39 0243353521, servizi@civita.it). It is possible to join an existing group or else pay the full price of the ticket. | **Tip** In front is the building designed by Mario Cucinella for Deloitte, its double-skin glazing a perfect example of an innovative bioclimatic solution used to upgrade an old building.

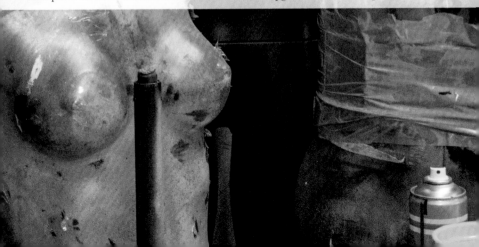

111_WOW

Make way for the comic books

The grayness of the large avenue clashes with the colorful mural painted on the wall outside the gardens, which depicts Pluto, Mickey Mouse, Diabolik, and a host of other comic characters, not to mention the big blue arch covered in white clouds that dominates the entrance. A large speech bubble reads "WOW" in red capital letters. Welcome to the Milan comics museum, aptly located in a former *panettone* factory (that would have pleased Grandma Duck).

The park is filled with fantastical sculptures, like the cheery Loch Ness-style monster that rises up next to the skate park where the kids whizz by at breakneck speed. In Italy, comic books – the ninth art – are still underappreciated, despite this being the birthplace of many famous illustrators, such as Gian Luigi Bonelli (Tex Willer's "father") and Hugo Pratt. The *Corriere dei Piccoli*, the first Italian periodical to make a regular feature of comic strips, was launched in 1908.

WOW is also a space where children and adults can come together to participate in various workshops or simply browse the shelves for their favorite comic books, from *Dragon Ball* to old editions of *Mickey Mouse.*

Many internationally renowned comic-book artists have left their mark here, such as the Chilean artist Eduardo Carrasco, nicknamed "Moro," who painted a mural of Paperinik (Donald Duck's heroic alter ego, known as "Duck Avenger" in English) next to the outdoor cafe, Boom.

WOW is run by the Fossati Foundation, which has a historical archive of thousands of books, comics, films, original illustrated panels, and merchandise that are now considered to be collectors' items. These are often presented to the public within the framework of themed exhibitions, which are organized on the first floor. WOW offers an unusual way to get in sync with our fantasies: through the adventures of so many characters that have filled our imaginations.

Address Viale Campania 12, 20133 Milan, Tel. +39 0249524744, www.museowow.it |
Getting there Porta Vittoria (Passante Ferroviario); Campania/Corsica (tram 27;
bus 73, 90, 91, 93); Mugello/Campania (bus 45) | Hours Tue–Fri 3–7pm, Sat–Sun
3–8pm | Tip At Viale Campania 51 is the Spazio 900 showroom, which offers interior
design objects in vintage 1950s–1970s style (Mon–Sat 3:30–7:30pm).

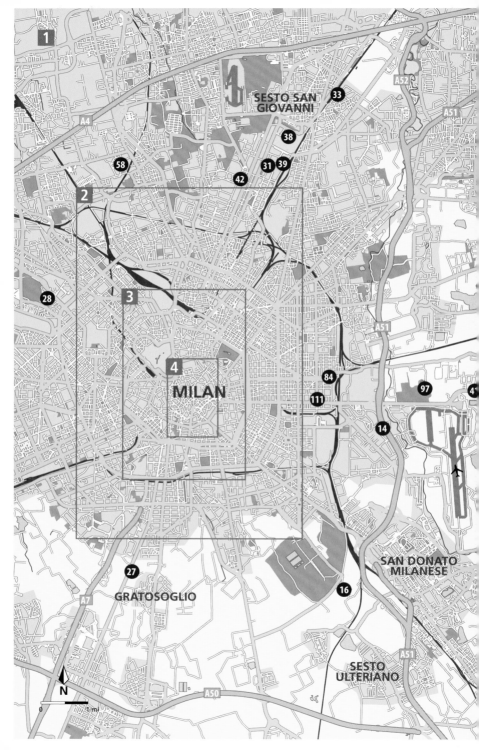

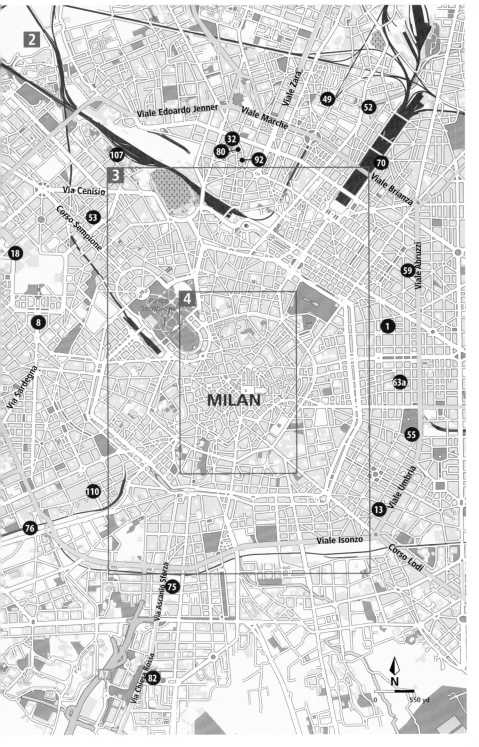

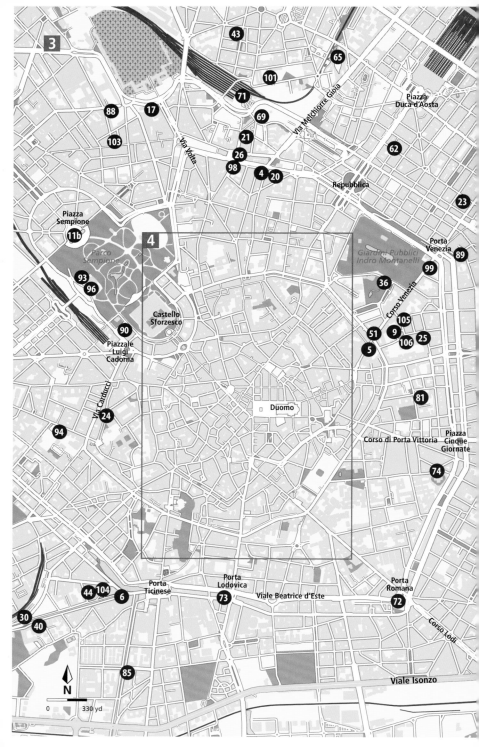

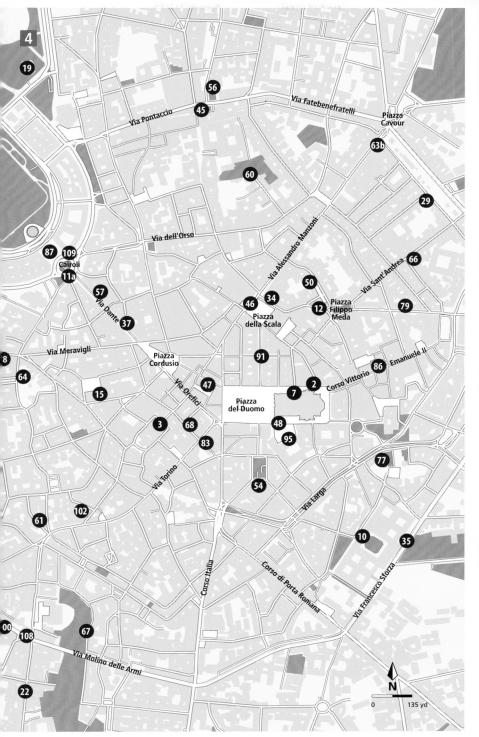

Lucia Jay von Seldeneck,
Carolin Huder, Verena Eidel
**111 PLACES IN BERLIN
THAT YOU SHOULDN'T MISS**
ISBN 978-3-95451-208-9

Rüdiger Liedtke
**111 PLACES IN MUNICH
THAT YOU SHOULDN'T MISS**
ISBN 978-3-95451-222-5

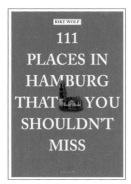

Rike Wolf
**111 PLACES IN HAMBURG
THAT YOU SHOULDN'T MISS**
ISBN 978-3-95451-234-8

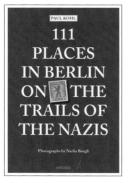

Paul Kohl
**111 PLACES IN BERLIN
ON THE TRAIL OF THE NAZIS**
ISBN 978-3-95451-323-9

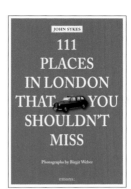

John Sykes
**111 PLACES IN LONDON
THAT YOU SHOULDN'T MISS**
ISBN 978-3-95451-346-8

Dirk Engelhardt
**111 PLACES IN BARCELONA
THAT YOU MUST NOT MISS**
ISBN 978-3-95451-353-6

Peter Eickhoff
**111 PLACES IN VIENNA
THAT YOU SHOULDN'T MISS**
ISBN 978-3-95451-206-5

Stefan Spath
**111 PLACES IN SALZBURG
THAT YOU SHOULDN'T MISS**
ISBN 978-3-95451-230-0

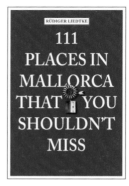

Rüdiger Liedtke
**111 PLACES ON MALLORCA
THAT YOU SHOULDN'T MISS**
ISBN 978-3-95451-281-2

Marcus X. Schmid
**111 PLACES IN ISTANBUL
THAT YOU MUST NOT MISS**
ISBN 978-3-95451-423-6

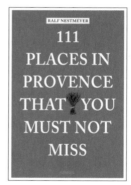

Ralf Nestmeyer
**111 PLACES IN PROVENCE
THAT YOU MUST NOT MISS**
ISBN 978-3-95451-422-9

Christiane Bröcker,
Babette Schröder
**111 PLACES IN STOCKHOLM
THAT YOU MUST NOT MISS**
ISBN 978-3-95451-459-5

Gerd Wolfgang Sievers
**111 PLACES IN VENICE
THAT YOU MUST NOT MISS**
ISBN 978-3-95451-460-1

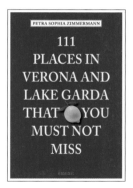

Petra Sophia Zimmermann
**111 PLACES IN VERONA
AND LAKE GARDA THAT
YOU MUST NOT MISS**
ISBN 978-3-95451-611-7

Annett Klingner
**111 PLACES IN ROME
THAT YOU MUST NOT MISS**
ISBN 978-3-95451-469-4

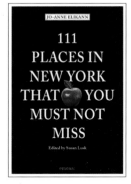

Jo-Anne Elikann
**111 PLACES IN NEW YORK
THAT YOU MUST NOT MISS**
ISBN 978-3-95451-052-8

We thank the Venerable Fabbrica del Duomo, the Biblioteca Ambrosiana, the Soprintendenza ai Beni Archeologici della Regione Lombardia and Comune di Milano, the city's museums, the Cimitero Monumentale, the Fondo Ambiente Italiano FAI, and all who were involved in the creation of this book.

Journalist **Giulia Castelli Gattinara** and photographer **Mario Verin** share their lives, their work, and their love for travel. Their essays have appeared in the most important Italian magazines and newspapers (*Geo, Bell'Italia, La Repubblica, La Stampa*, and many others). Both are mountain climbers, which provides them with a very special view of the world – and of Milan, where they have been living for 25 years.